Alfre Quiñones-Hinojosa

Biography

From Migrant Worker to World-Renowned Neurosurgeon

Paresa H Alizadeh

TABLE OF CONTENTS

Part I Stargazing

1. Starry Nights

2. Faraway

3. The Kaliman Maneuver

4. Lessons from the Fields

Part II Harvesting

5. Courting Destiny

6. Question the Rules and When Possible Make Your Own

Part III Becoming Dr. Q

7. Hopkins

8. Gray Matter

9. Seeing the Light

10. Finding the Steel in Your Soul

PART I: STARGAZING

April 14, 1989, near the port of Stockton, California, I was 21 years old, the eldest son of Sostenes and Flavia Quiñones, working at California Railcar Repair as a welder, painter and driver. On an ordinary morning, my colleague Pablo and I were removing the covers of giant compressed air tanks. Even though we knew there was gas left in the tank, we did not wear protective masks. While working, an iron screw fell into the sink, so I decided to climb down with a rope to get it back. As I climbed down, the gas affected me, making me dizzy and unconscious.

I realized there was no more air in the tub and started to climb up, but it felt heavy and difficult due to lack of oxygen. While trying to overcome fear and despair, I gradually lost my hearing and eyesight, and could only focus on climbing. My father, Sostenes, also worked there and ran to help after hearing cries for help. When Pablo ran to pull me, I completely lost consciousness, slipped out of Pablo's arms and fell to the bottom of the tub.

1. Starry Nights

During the many minutes I lay at the bottom of the tank without oxygen, struggling on the battleground between life and death, the image of laying on my back, enveloped in darkness and staring up at the light struck a profound chord with me. Indeed, as I travel back down memory's tiny pathways to the farthest past, the first image that rises to greet me is the familiar, starry night sky.

I spent many of the warmest evenings of the year up on the roof of our little house on the outskirts of the tiny community of Palaco, in the northern portion of Mexico's Baja peninsula. I would frequently lie awake for hours observing the limitless expanse of blackest outer space, which was illuminated by a gorgeous moon and millions of beautiful, sparkling, dancing stars. Many of life's most urgent concerns were initially seeded in my mind beneath the panoramic dome-along with my high degree of curiosity and thirst for adventure. I may also find relief from the weight of daily problems and other worries under the stars whenever melancholy or unexpected catastrophe strikes.

Such was the nature of my earliest, most vivid memory, which was of an occurrence that occurred when I was three years old. The trauma was caused by one of my siblings, Maricela, who I will always remember for her wide brown laughing eyes and round, chubby, smiling face. When I returned home after playing one morning, she was nowhere to be found.

We were living in the two rear rooms of my father's gas station at the time. When I came into our living quarters' kitchen area that morning, I felt a horrible grief in the air. The day was overcast, muggy, and very cold. In the kitchen, where my mother, Flavia, was sitting, strange yellow vinyl chairs had been set. Mamá, a charming, small woman who was generally cheerful, was sobbing as she cradled Maricela's twin, Rosa, five months old, to breastfeed her. Gabriel, my two-year-old brother, was by her side. Gabriel licked his thumb gently as he leaned against our sobbing mother, gazing around with his huge, intelligent eyes. A tiny rectangular wooden box-a casket, I later learned-sat in front of the yellow chairs, wrapped by a colourful handwoven blanket. Family members and neighbours entered the room, many of them sobbing silently.

When I asked my aunt why Mamá was so upset, she revealed that it was my baby sister Maricela's death.

"Where is Maricela?" I muttered, unable to make the connection between my cheerful, fat baby sister and the casket.

"Maricela went to heaven," my mother replied gravely as she wiped away her tears.

Why was everyone so depressed? After all, I'd heard that paradise was a beautiful place where people might go to be with the angels. Shouldn't we be happy that she went to such a wonderful place?

Years later, I learnt the awful circumstances surrounding Maricela's death: acute diarrhoea and dehydration, a common and curable ailment if the proper medical services are available. She wasn't sent to the hospital at first since we lived in the middle of nowhere with no close services. The difficulty in obtaining medical assistance was due to the relative poverty in this rural location outside of Palaco, a little village of around 500 people about thirty miles from Mexicali- the border town divided by a fence and known as Calexico on the US side. There were no private doctors who made house calls in our village or nearby, nor were there clinics. The boticas housed in local pharmacies met many of the day-to-day medical needs. My mother took Maricela to the botica when her symptoms first manifested, and the pharmacist offered Mamá medicine to relieve the baby's stomach troubles and suffering, which was eventually identified as colitis.

Maricela began to chuckle as my father scooped her up in his arms when he returned home from work that evening. Papá interpreted her smiles as proof that the treatment was working. My parents rushed Maricela over to my grandmother, Nana Maria, my father's mother, a curandera who specialised as a midwife and herbalist, in the middle of the night, as her screams escalated from what was plainly tremendous pain. My grandmother had delivered hundreds of babies over the years and was respected for her ability to recognize when a case required extra care. Nana realised right away that Maricela needed to be rushed to the seguro social-the public hospital-without delay. My parents saw the gravity of the situation and rushed to the scene.

At the hospital, one of the doctors on duty recognized my grandma and responded to her anxiety by admitting my little sister right away and assuring my parents that she would be OK by morning. Mamá and Papá then had the agony of witnessing Maricela's convulsions worsen over the next two days, and eventually losing daughter. They did everything they could, but it wasn't enough to fight her colitis, which had fast progressed, or to compensate for the fact that the small, underfunded hospital didn't have the medicine or other forms of care that could have saved her. Unfortunately, in underdeveloped nations like ours, diarrhoea and dehydration remain the leading causes of death among children. But I know my parents kept asking themselves Why?, and the issue lingered over the family for years.

My father and mother had both experienced loss. My father was one of eleven children, one of them died at the age of ten before my father was born, casting a long shadow on that family. My mother had been virtually orphaned at the age of six when her beloved mother died in childbirth, essentially leaving her to raise the younger children while her father, my grandfather Jesus, struggled to find his footing after his wife's death.

Though my parents never expressed their grief publicly, it remained a constant in our lives, an undercurrent of loss that affected each of us individually. I believe my sister's death was caused by the increased sense of responsibility I felt as the oldest of five children in our family, as well as recurring childhood nightmares in which I would find myself in the midst of a disaster-0fire, flood, or avalanche-and realise it was up to me to save my mother and siblings. In each of these dreams, I was given superpowers, such as the ability to walk across fire without being burned or swim through tidal waves without drowning (in reality, I couldn't swim and would never be at peace in the water). The idea of possessing extraordinary abilities must have stemmed from my desire to emulate Kaliman, a Mexican comic-book superhero who could repel numerous demon attacks with a single move: the gravity-defying Kaliman manoeuvre, which I was determined to learn one day. During my waking hours, I was confident that I could do it. But, in my nightmares, before I could use my superpowers to save my loved ones, the dream would come to an end and I would fail in my goal. I'd wake up crying in baffled frustration every time.

Maricela's death, my recurring nightmares, and the sense of responsibility I felt from a young age may help explain why my most primordial quest was to understand and make meaning of life and death. These encounters may have also sowed the seeds of my later interest in medicine. Meanwhile, the thought that my sister had gone to a better place was reassuring. It strengthened my already active imagination and my desire to learn more about the world beyond what I could see and observe in the daily comings and goings on Palaco's outskirts. I dreamed of a life of travel and adventure long before medicine was even a realistic possibility for me!

However, as I recollect my nights of stargazing when I was six and a half, almost seven years old, I was content to be an astronaut. One swelteringly hot autumn night in 1974, I told my mother, my five-year-old brother Gabriel, and my three-year-old sister Rosa about my plan.

Everyone burst out laughing. I was unquestionably the family daydreamer!

There were many nights like this one when the oppressive heat inside our two-bedroom house, where we had relocated a year before, made sleep difficult. The adobe-style house, built of cinder blocks in one section and mud in the other, was just across the canal from the gas station and lacked air conditioning, roasting everything inside! When the heat became oppressive, as it did this night, the four of us climbed up to the rooftop, first laying blankets across the rough tar-paper surface, then getting into position. Rosa sat on one side of Mamá, and I sat on the other, between her and Gabriel. We took to the roof not just to escape the heat, but also to avoid the ever-present threat of earthquakes, which have been known to topple houses and cause mudslides in this section of Baja, where the San Andreas Fault runs down from the west coast of the United States. You were more likely to survive up on the roof if the house didn't fall on you, as had lately happened in the region, killing hundreds. But those concerns appeared to dissipate under the stars, where everything was safe, serene, and enjoyable!

I fashioned a pillow for myself by clasping my hands beneath my head, and with my legs crossed, I was at ease-happily engaged and ready to relish the performance taking place in the sky above us and in our surroundings.

We remained quiet for a time. We didn't say anything as our senses became aware of the sights, sounds, and smells of the night. I could hear crickets chirping and other insects buzzing, as well as the loud croaking of toads who sang with a bravado reminiscent of the strolling mariachis who visited Mexicali's eateries.

During these years, we were lucky to eat out occasionally and to be part of our village's lower middle class, gradually rising out of poverty thanks to my father's modest earnings from his gas station. While our situation was more hazardous than we realised, I recognized that the rungs on the ladder were numerous. I was also aware that not every family could afford to eat meat once a week like we did, and that none of our good fortune would have been possible without the family work ethic. This fundamental lesson had been instilled in me since the age of five, when I went to work at the gas station every day after school and on weekends, pumping gas, learning to fix automobiles and trucks, and even driving them in and out of our mechanic's garage with the assistance of numerous cushions. I saw nothing strange about being a five-year-old who could drive or climb up on hydraulic lifts to inspect the undercarriages of vehicles and trucks to see what needed to be repaired-it was all part of the job.

My family taught me the value of hard work both directly and by example. My father began his day at the gas station at daybreak and worked until late at night, when he went out to spend some of the day's profits on food and other needs for the family. As a result, he wasn't always on the roof when we went up there to sleep. But I knew that when he got home later, he'd have something for all of us to eat in the morning, usually a loaf of pan dulce, or sweet bread.

On this night in my recollection, I envisioned with pleasure what breakfast would bring, even as I absorbed the night's green, damp, soil smells, savouring it all. Everything was new, present, and living, like the scent of freshly harvested watermelon pulled from the moist soil, ripe and ready to eat. How well I remembered these odours from recent trips to labour in Palaco's cotton fields. Though our efforts were not required for money at this time, my parents felt that we would apply what we learned in the fields in other ways. Papá also wanted to teach me that working at the gas station was a far better job than standing in the hot sun all day picking cotton with my bare hands.

It was pointless to complain out in the field. So I made the best of the situation by observing the process as we walked up and down the rows, collecting the light fluffy pieces of cotton and placing them in long burlap sacks, and then witnessing how the filled-up sacks were weighed so that we could get paid by the kilogram. There was no shame in working in the field. This was a golden opportunity. In addition, I was proud of what I could do with my bare hands. The moral of the story was twofold: first, every job in the entire operation was important job was meaningless; second, no matter how small and fluffy that piece of cotton felt, if we kept pushing forward, all those bits of fluff would accumulate and have real weight-as much as twenty or thirty kilos worth their weight in pesos!

Such was the importance of honest, tough effort, which brought with it the satisfaction of a job well done, some form of pay, and occasionally possibilities to advance in life. This is how I ended up buying the old bike I sorely needed. When I brought home the bike, Gabriel, a much more disciplined child than I who also had more common sense, was unimpressed. "How can you ride it?" he chuckled, pointing out the lack of pedals and brakes. I learned to ride it sideways and generally roll anywhere the bicycle wanted to go to prove him wrong.

Gabriel, on the other hand, was much more enthusiastic when the two of us found a used black-and-white RCA television in a thrift store and convinced our father to buy it-though he was careful to point out that we only had one line of power to the house, which was needed for the refrigerator and the two light bulbs that lit our home. Unfazed, we constructed a temporary outlet that provided us with enough power. When we replaced the image tube, the picture appeared mysteriously, exciting us-at least for the few hours that Mexican television broadcasted the two available stations.

We covered the windows with blankets to darken the rooms because the TV image was quite fuzzy. With temperatures outside reaching 120 degrees, the insulation simply served to make the indoors feel hotter. But we didn't mind! The television was a luxury item that not only connected us to the rest of the globe, but also to the amazing possibilities of space flight to strange new worlds. We were hooked on Star Trek repeats in the afternoons, raptly following Dr. Spock and Captain Kirk as they roamed the galaxies, battling dangers, fighting wars, dodging asteroids, and delving into unexplored realms.

There was one major issue. When being so diligent and inventive in repairing the television set, I was unable to view it since I had to work at the gas station when my father picked us up from school at midday. Unfortunately, this meant that I could only watch Star Trek on a catch-as-catch-can basis. I remember being eager to watch an episode that was scheduled to air at 4:30 p.m. on a Thursday afternoon. When Papá picked me up from school and I begged if he might make an exception for this day, he said flatly, "No, Alfredo, you have to work," and left it at that.

I was heartbroken. However, I did not cry. Instead, when we got to the gas station, I sprang out of the car, set my jaw, and went about my chores with renewed zeal, hoping to forget about the Star Trek episode I was bound to miss. I had almost succeeded in pushing it to the back of my mind by the time four-thirty rolled around. Papá then called me over and motioned toward home, saying, "OK, son, you can go to the house," and before he could add, "and watch your show," I raced out the door as fast as my small legs could take me.

When I walked in, Gabriel informed me that I had just missed the opening credits, and we were able to marvel together as the USS Enterprise set sail into the unknown. The episode exceeded my expectations in every way! And on that hot autumn night in 1974, sitting there on the rooftop with Gabriel, Mamá, and Rosa, I knew that someday, just like Captain Kirk did in that episode, I could land on a hostile planet and utilise my diplomacy abilities to keep the peace. I basked in the main event, which was already underway, energised by the sounds of the wind in the shrubbery of the foothills to the north of us. I liked the fast stars-the ones that were the smallest but seemed to be on a specific mission, moving with purpose and power. Amazing! Millions of stories and possibilities presented themselves on the enormous whiteboard above us to the would-be astronaut in my six-year-old self.

In the second grade, I was developing a feeling of geography. I'd heard that Palaco, which stood for Pacific Land business, was formed by a long-gone American business that came in about the 1930s to develop the valley's diverse crops. I also knew that we were a satellite village, like many others in Mexicali, and that there were other, much larger cities far away in the vast country of Mexico, of which I was a citizen. We had learned about countries and continents, as well as their geographical differences. Whereas I had previously believed that the globe was flat and that if I reached the end, I would fall off the edge, I now understood from school and Star Trek that the earth was round-and was stationed in the cosmos much like a star. Aside from those fundamentals, I only had questions: What lay beyond the heavens? What was it between the stars and the blackness that separated them? Who made them? My mind couldn't fathom where this immense expanse began or ended, or how it could be quantified in relation to me, such a small entity in the grand scheme.

Tata Juan, my paternal grandfather, was the only other person who seemed to be thinking about such mysteries. In fact, he was instrumental in sowing the seeds of these major issues in my mind, encouraging me on to greater heights. "If you shoot high and aim for a star, you might just hit one," he said.

I once followed his counsel seriously when I was around five years old. I took my slingshot and a handful of stones up to the roof one night and did exactly what he said, shooting each one as far into the sky as I could. Although I didn't strike a star that night, I was confident that I would one day.

According to family members, I kept everyone on their toes from the minute I was born on January 2, 1968. First and foremost, a strange bulge on my head sparked suspicions that I had been born with a brain tumour. I now know that I had a cephalohematoma, which was nothing significant. Family members puzzled how I survived the fist-sized bulge rising from my skull-composed of broken blood vessels-which appeared to be a second tiny head attempting to push its way through the skin.

After learning that the bump would go away on its own, family members focused their attention on my energetic personality, fearing that I would injure myself. My parents were astounded by how quickly I could toddle away even before I could walk well. By my first birthday, I had also learned to speak expressively and had taught myself to tie my shoelaces. The true trouble started now. My disappearances frequently prompted the entire extended family to go out and look for me, such as when I was about three years old and everyone thought I'd fallen into the reservoir. They ultimately tracked me down and spotted me selling the little shrimp I'd discovered in irrigation holes in the fields. My numerous uncles found these shenanigans amusing, but my numerous aunts did not. They quickly called me a hellion in desperate need of better discipline. My parents did their best, but it wasn't enough. Nana Maria predicted that if they didn't create some form of boundaries for me, I'd end up hurting myself. Tata Juan, who took me under his wing and became my first true mentor, took over the role.

Tata was a towering figure for all of us, tall and lanky, with chiselled features and an eagle's beak for a nose. Despite never having attended school, he learnt to read and write music while also training himself to play numerous instruments. Tata also made a few clever investments during his years toiling in agriculture (as we used to call working in the fields), and he carried himself with such regal bearing that he could have been mistaken for a nobleman throughout his life. As a gentleman, he was never without his hat-a show of dignity, I believe-and he never failed to take it off in front of ladies.

"How are you today, my ladies?" he'd ask, sweeping his hat off and bowing anytime he passed a group of women of any age. Even though I didn't wear a hat, I imitated this mannerism as a child. I liked it when I bowed and said, in my best five-year-old pronunciation, "How are you today, my ladies?" I've done that ever since because it worked so wonderfully!

My favourite recollections of my granddad are from our vacations to the Rumorosa Mountains. Everything about the area amazed me, from the massive, rocky mountain peaks to the mystery labyrinth of caves with archaic wall paintings left by old human hands. Tata defied his age and raced like a gazelle up the trekking routes that climbed up the mountains. On purpose, he would speed off into the woods, forcing me to think quickly and chase him into the thicket. There were moments when he'd vanish, and just as I was about to panic, Tata would resurface and we'd continue up the steep mountain together, far from the main trail.

On one occasion, he put our hikes' lessons into words. "Alfredo, whenever you have a choice, don't just follow where the path leads," he added, placing his hand on my shoulder as we climbed. Instead, go where there is no route and create a trail." I'm not sure if Tata has heard a similar phrase by Ralph Waldo Emerson. However, I wouldn't be surprised if he did.

Tata Juan would not sit down to relax until we reached the rocky peak. Then he'd smile while I ran around, screaming at the top of my lungs, "Tata Aaaahhhh! Tata Aaaahhhh!" and enjoying the sound as it echoed down the slope.

My parents must have been relieved when the two of us returned from our adventures in one piece, even if they never said anything. I'm sure they were relieved that we were so near. However, not everyone expressed their emotions. Tata seemed to spend more time with me than with anyone else, according to one of my father's sisters, out of his fifty-two grandkids, some of whom were senior to me. Papá undoubtedly advised that having someone in the family who could control me would be beneficial!

My mother frequently used Tata as a go-between when she needed to explain to me why I had to bear the consequences of breaking the rules. I would argue against the penalty, whether it was to sit in the corner or to stop watching television, telling Mamá that she was being too tough. Tata would ask me to tell him the complete story about my indiscretions, whether I skipped chores or got into a fight, and then pass judgement. That's what occurred one day when my mother was unhappy with me because I was playing on the railroad lines behind our house. (Incidentally, these rails were part of the line that carried freight trains and railway tankers from Northern California. The train carriages that went through my yard were the same tankers that I would one day clean and refurbish—thus putting my life in danger.)

I used to offer to assist the switching guards and engineers as a child because they couldn't move as quickly as I could. My task was to stand by the side of the tracks until the last possible moment to determine whether the locomotive needed the track switched and, if so, leap over the track while signalling the guards and engineers to pull the proper levers at the appropriate time. This was, in my opinion, educational and wonderful training in my goal to become an astronaut or a superhero like Kaliman. My mother was adamantly opposed.

On the day in question, Tata requested me to explain a specific occurrence and explain why my work as a switching guard required me to climb up on a tanker car that had only stopped briefly, forcing me to jump when it quickly started moving again. "Your mother is absolutely correct, Alfredo," he said slowly and severely after hearing me defend myself and a few additional details. You may have been murdered. You set a poor example for the other kids. "I believe you should think about this as you sit in the corner." He had just said practically word for word what my mother had said! But when he said them, I agreed wholeheartedly. The punishment was no longer excessive. Indeed, I considered it an honour to face my penalties at his request.

One of the reasons I admired Tata was his ability to overcome the challenges he had endured throughout his life. His father was slain by a band of pistoleros-lawless, thieving gangs who ravaged the countryside during the Mexican Revolution-when he was a child in Sonora, where he was born in 1907. His mother later had mental illness, making life even more difficult for my grandfather, who reared himself.

Nana Maria had also endured a great deal of adversity. Though I wasn't as close to her as I was to Tata, I admired her job as a healer and community leader. Her job as a curandera taught me the most crucial thing I would learn about patient treatment and care: the patient's life and well-being must always come first. Nana had a gift for connecting with her patients in an instant, tactile way, gazing into their eyes, scrutinising their slightest symptoms, and placing her hands on their shoulders to encourage and share her tremendous healing energy. Nobody died in her care because she was so thorough that if she had any doubts about whether someone needed more than she could supply, she would refer the patient to a hospital or facility that could. Nana Maria never asked for a single peso in exchange for her services. Her reward was being able to teach women how to care for their reproductive health and their kids, and as a midwife, she felt it an honour to save lives and assist in the birth of new life. That, she thought, made for a richly rewarding life. She would stay awake and alert throughout protracted periods of labour and difficult deliveries, standing and working through the cold nights in our area's small unheated adobe homes or the suffocating hot nights when everyone else fled to their roofs for relief.

When I was around six years old, on a hot July morning after a long delivery, I saw Nana Maria on her front porch while I was playing outside my grandparents' house. Despite resting her legs and feet, Nana appeared unexpectedly fresh and revitalised after a sleepless night as a midwife. She walked with a limp, which my father explained was due to a disability or sickness, such as polio, that had caused one foot to be far smaller than the other. My grandmother never complained, even when she and Tata were working in the fields. Nana did believe, however, that too many of us took the magnificent ability bestowed upon us by the strength of our own two feet for granted. And she never shied away from appreciating someone else's gorgeous gait or expressing a forlorn longing to have two regular feet and even dance like others. Perhaps her sense of otherness made her more empathetic to others in pain and struggle. But, when I was playing with my cousin Cesar-a rock throwing master who was helping me improve my technique-I sensed something magical about Nana Maria. Instead of looking tired, she was smiling and conversing with Tata, as if energised. It was wonderful to have so much stamina after going so long without eating or sleeping, and to do so while caring for others was a very noble gesture.

Just then, a young couple walked down the road toward my grandparents' house, as if on cue. While her husband clutched a live chicken in his arms, the young mother carried her newborn baby under a cover. I was impressed by the young mother and father's expressions of gratitude as they presented my grandmother with the chicken, the most valuable gift they could locate to express their gratitude. Nana Maria was cordial, assuring them that their kindness would not go unnoticed in her modest home. Perhaps the most valuable present she received was the opportunity to look under the cover and see the healthy tiny baby, knowing she had done her job successfully.

The story had a twist that made it memorable for another reason. I decided to put my new talents to the test once the young couple left and Nana went inside. The first rock flew out of my hands at breakneck speed. Unfortunately, my aim was poor, and I shattered a window in my grandparents' house. Guacamole for days! But, not giving up, I tossed the next rock, taking care to avoid the house. Unfortunately, I wasn't careful enough this time to avoid hitting Cesar's head, resulting in a gash that bled profusely as his screams chased my grandparents away.

Nana pointed out that I had demonstrated yet again that I needed to be more conscious of my actions. Tata was quite dissatisfied. Of course, I was upset about my cousin and the window. Above all, I didn't want my grandparents to be upset with me. They weren't, in fact, though they were concerned. My grandma told my parents that I would go far in life provided suitable boundaries were placed, I subsequently learnt. Tata Juan forewarned Papa. "Alfredo has an unusually bright personality. But you must keep an eye on him. Otherwise, he will pass up numerous opportunities." My parents agreed wholeheartedly. Rather than being unduly critical, their answer was to ensure that I settled down through education and classroom discipline. Because neither of my parents had any formal schooling, the necessity for me and my siblings to go to school, work hard in the classroom and on homework, and make the most of our education was all the more important to my parents.

My maternal grandmother had taught my mother to read and write at home before she died. In fact, one of my mother's sole memories of this time was seeing my grandmother's warm smile of approval while they read together. But, after being orphaned and forced to work as a servant by her aunts, my mother had little choice but to educate herself. Despite these constraints, Mamá performed admirably and was able to apply the fundamentals in qualifying for a training program to become a nurse, her lifelong ambition. Unfortunately, her father, my grandfather Jesus, refused to assist her in paying for nursing school. Nonetheless, Mamá continued to educate herself, gaining skills that she eventually put to use when she went into business, purchasing used products that she would restore and then sell.

My father was thirteen years old the first time his family relocated near enough to a school for him to attend. But, being the oldest student in the class and the only one with facial hair, he felt like a swarthy giant. Despite learning enough to later teach himself to read and write, he only stayed in class for three months before dropping out. Nobody was more dissatisfied than he was. Papá would later advise us, regretting that he hadn't been able to achieve everything he desired in life, "If you want to grow up and be like me, don't go to school."

My parents had pondered finishing their schooling when they married in 1967, but with babies to feed and a petrol station to run, they never had time. When Tata was in his late teens, my father took over the firm. "Sostenes, I've been thinking about buying the Garcia Gas Station that's for sale," Juan stated. Do you want to be my partner?" Then, as a wedding gift, Tata approached my father and said, "The gas station has always been yours, son." "I knew you'd need it when you started a family."

Papa only wanted to make his father proud-to prove himself worthy. That mission proved to be more difficult than he had anticipated. However, in accordance with Tata's expectations, my father devoted himself to making the business a huge success, quickly changing the average gas station into a colourful, eye-catching operation. Because he likes bright colours, he painted it a neon mustard yellow with bright lime green trim. It was impossible to overlook!

My father passed on his love of colour to me. But his most essential legacy was his oft-repeated line, delivered with a smile or tears in his eyes: "Every man is the architect of his own destiny."

Tata Juan believed that charm and charisma could carry a person a long way, and that when combined with hard effort, honesty, and a decent heart, you could go "a long way and back." He also felt that great things might arise from tiny efforts. He gave me my first marble as proof, stating, "If you use this well, you will have more marbles than you can count in time." Tata was spot on. I quickly became the king of marbles, organising tournaments that I oversaw while working at the gas station. Thus began my training in multitasking, an essential talent for me as a future clinician, surgeon, and scientist. Untold numbers of jars packed with marbles of all colours soon lined the nooks and crannies of our tiny home.

My desire to win all the marbles, a competitive instinct that would bring me into problems later, worked against me when I was drawn into a competition with a nine-year-old competitor when I was six. While he was letting me win, his elder buddy crept into the station and took fifty pesos! I had no choice but to avenge myself in the face of such cold-blooded deception. But, having tried before and been kicked in the shins by older youngsters, I decided it was time to establish an entourage-a long-lasting tradition. My team was made up of former bullies who I had become friends with. I brought the brain; they brought the muscle.

However, I did not back down from the fight. After all, I was still practising as Kaliman, convinced that I could perfect the manoeuvre he used to fight off multiple opponents at once. After closely studying the comic book version, I realised that in order to pull off the manoeuvre properly, I would need to emulate Kaliman's green-eyed, pantherlink quickness by jumping five feet into the air while extending my arms and legs. The goal was to knock out four opponents by striking them with my fists and kicking them with my feet. I'd disarm them with lightning quickness and then fall on my feet again, like a panther. It was also critical, I thought, that my eyes burned with defiance, much as Kaliman's eyes turned a more vivid shade of green whenever he fought demons.

"I'm going to practise the Kaliman manoeuvre, and I need your help," I told Gabriel and three of my cousins. Do precisely what I say, and you won't be too injured."

Seeing their anxiety, I reminded them of the trouble we were experiencing with local bullies who were wandering the area and shooting BB guns at us. In case of an attack, we had to practise the manoeuvre ahead of time.

We all took our seats, bracing ourselves for the onslaught. I concentrated, inhaled deeply, bowed my knees, and sprang into the air, ascending little more than two feet. I extended my arms and legs at the same moment, intending to punch and kick at the same time, but instead landed face down in the dirt, knocking the air out of my chest. Talk about consuming dust! When I sat up on my haunches, the four of them looked at me in fear and disgust at my failure. Then they started laughing hysterically.

What is my conclusion? Clearly, the comic book inflated Kaliman's abilities! As the tougher students continued to cause problems for the rest of us, I began to explore new ways to disarm the bullies.

Even as a supposed hellion, I managed to get through childhood with only one doctor visit. On this particular occasion, the pain and infection in my bicep grew so severe that I had to admit that I had landed on one of the drumsticks I'd constructed to go with the drum setup I'd assembled. The jagged wooden point of the drumstick had penetrated my arm, breaking off in the right bicep. It amazed me that the doctor could check my infected injury and, like a wizard, extract the piece of wood from my bicep and administer the appropriate medication to make everything better. Magic!

Although I considered being a doctor to be a worthy pursuit, my first true role model was Mexico's adored Benito Pablo Juárez Garca. When I started kindergarten, my teacher discovered that I already knew how to read and chose me to recite a poem about him in front of a crowd of hundreds of pupils. This was my first opportunity to speak in public, and I was frightened! To talk, I had to stand on a chair, and the microphone had to be lowered and turned sideways so I could reach it. On the stone wall high above me, I could see a quotation by Benito Juárez: "Among individuals, as among nations, when there is respect, there is peace." This energised me, and when I began to talk, I forgot about the audience and focused my energy on paying tribute to Juárez-a poor young man of indigenous descent who grew up to become Mexico's president. He epitomised real-life heroism, fighting for ordinary people.

School, as my parents intended, provided me with structure with defined boundaries from the start, allowing me to excel. At home, I could break the rules with my experiments and explorations, allowing my curiosity to run wild. School was a new type of fun, full of difficulties and excitement. There, I learned to be calm and concentrated, and as a result, I became the most obedient and disciplined student.

My father used to tell me about the time he came to pick me up from kindergarten and my teacher said, "I think Alfredo is ready for elementary school." You could talk to my sister and see what she says."

Fortunately for me, her sister, Senorita Jauregui, my first and second grade teacher, not only decided that I was ready for primary school, but also took me under her wing right away. She believed in my ability to succeed in school and in life. I quickly became the teacher's pet, which was both an honour and an invitation for other students to beat me up on the playground and after school. It was bad enough that I was younger and smaller than the other pupils in my grade. On top of that, I was from outside of town, a rural bumpkin in the perspective of Palaco's city people. I would have been in big trouble if it hadn't been for my street-smart closest friend, Niki, my enormous sidekick. My would-be assailants quickly realised that if they messed with me, they'd have to mess with him or one of the tougher youngsters I befriended. Despite my defenders, I continued to see myself as the underdog and identified with others who were bullied, especially those who couldn't defend themselves.

One day, a small boy in my second-grade class, also named Alfredo, raised his hand to beg to go to the restroom, which prompted me to become especially unhappy. He was told to wait until class was finished. Unfortunately, he couldn't control himself and pooped in his trousers. Alfredo was devastated. I felt terrible for him and was humiliated for his sake when the other kids began to tease him. I decided to ridicule those kids for their numerous flaws as soon as we got to the schoolyard, hurling sharp-tongued remarks that came naturally to me. Fighting for his cause wouldn't solve everything for the other Alfredo, but I hoped it would cheer him up.

I'll never forget a young girl in the region who was born with a disfiguring cleft palate that gave her the appearance of having two faces-"like a little monster," others claimed. Because they were impoverished, a few family members charged admission for others to come and stare at her, even shrieking over her deformities and taunting her. I couldn't stand by and watch such cruelty, even if it meant fighting with youngsters who were bigger than me. Most of the time, I lost those fights. But I hoped the little child was aware that someone was advocating for her.

2. Faraway

Misfortune crept quietly, almost invisibly, into my family's life at first. Then, around the end of 1977, when I was nine years old and in fifth grade, hard times seemed to descend on our family all at once, like a sudden change in the weather. Even through the cloudy prism of recollection, I recall the moment when I realized we had left the simpler, more secure days behind us and were stepping on shaky ground.

My revelation came when I discovered my father, alone and crying, behind our house. Something was horribly wrong. My initial thought was to inquire as to why Papá was crying. But I was too stunned to inquire. My father, the strong, obstinate head of our family, highly intellectual despite his lack of formal education, diligent, honest, and kind hearted, the colourful, passionate, larger-than-life man who was my hero, was bawling his eyes out.

There had been hints that things were not going well at the gas station for some time, but it wasn't until I discovered him crying that I realised the gravity of the situation. Without being told specifically, I deduced that the worst-case scenario for our family had occurred: the loss of the gas station, our principal source of income and way of putting food on the table. The station was our family's identity-not simply a place where I'd worked since I was five years old, but also a place of business that gave us clout in the neighbourhood. Even as a nine-year-old, I could see why this loss was such a blow to my father's self-esteem, not least because his father, Tata Juan, had chosen him to be his partner and then given him this endowment that was supposed to insure our future well-being.

In the year that followed, I had a clearer understanding of the events that had led to this situation. One aspect was Mexico's financial collapse, which would last several years and become a broad economic depression. We had steadily worked our way up to the lower middle class previously. But without the gas station, we fell so far off that rung that we had to fight for the simplest necessities, including the money needed to feed a growing family.

This slide shocked our system, as it did that of much of the country, which had been enjoying relative prosperity and improvement since the 1930s, when American corporations and other foreign investors came in to develop rural areas and outposts like Palaco. Outside investment helped to establish jobs and pull many people out of poverty. However, when enterprises departed (or were forced to leave when Mexican laws changed to limit foreign-owned business), jobs and family security were sometimes lost. The middle class plummeted, and the destitute became truly impoverished.

The other element that contributed to the gas station's demise was only discovered after my father had to sell it for close to nothing. To do so, he had to first give it to his brother, my uncle Jesus, in whose name the government had initially awarded the PEMEX (Petroleos Mexicanos) permit and who had carefully renewed it throughout the years—to his credit, given how few such permits were available nowadays. When Uncle Jesus attempted to hand over the gas station to new management, an inspection of the site uncovered an astonishing truth. Unbeknownst to Papá, holes in the gas tanks had been steadily seeping their contents into the earth all those years. Because so much gas had leaked from the underground tanks, everyone's first thought was to thank God that no stray lit match or mechanical explosion had created an inferno that would have devoured us all. We had been living in the flat in the back of the gas station for years, completely unaware that such a dreadful event-of the type that was all too usual in our area-could have occurred and taken our lives.

Why had it taken us so long to notice that we were paying more for gas than we were selling at the pumps? It should have been clearer that the earnings were practically oozing into the ground beneath our feet.

Distractions may have kept Papá from detecting our dwindling bottom line. And he was young and inexperienced, having never had the opportunity to travel the world before settling down, instead marrying at the age of twenty and becoming the father of six children within ten years. My father could have been suffering from depression, which grew more apparent as our financial situation deteriorated and drinking became a more common means of escape, a way to self-medicate.

Looking back, as I try to comprehend what my father went through, I genuinely believe he was destined for greatness, just as my grandfather said. But because Papá was not on solid ground when he was overturned, finding his way back to terra firma became even more difficult. Even though my aunts and uncles, as well as my paternal grandparents, maintained a policy of denial about how much trouble we were in, losing the gas station marked a loss in our position in the Quiones family and in the community. Despite our efforts to keep up appearances, they must have been aware of our difficulties.

But the reality couldn't be avoided in our house. It's difficult to be delusory when your stomach is empty. My mother stood over the stove, just flour and water and a touch of oil in the pan to feed us children-me at ten years old, Gabriel at almost nine, Rosa at seven years old, Jorge at about four years old, and baby Jaqueline not yet six months, then asleep for her nap. We sat at the table, hands folded, waiting calmly for the tortillas to come out of the pan. Decades later, I can vividly recall the aroma that warned us how good every piece would be. I can still hear the symphony of the tortilla sizzling in the oil when I recall that near quiet in the kitchen-the most hopeful sound in the world at the time. Even now, the simple mention of the term "hunger" brings that scene to mind.

Dinner was flour tortillas with homemade salsa. The days of eating meat only once a week were over. Gone were the nights when I imagined my father was out somewhere getting bread or something hearty for breakfast. Gone were the Christmas mornings when I awoke to the aroma of my mother's tamales. Instead of looking up at the sky and fantasising about journeying beyond the stars as I slept on the roof, I fantasised about more practical things, like a piece of pan dulce and a time when we could eat beans and potatoes again.

Every now and then, I'd have dreams about things I'd like to do or buy for myself that weren't tied to food or family, like the time I became obsessed with owning a pair of Ray-Ban sunglasses. They were the epitome of living la vida loca back then!

Strangely, it was during this darker period that the nightmares that had haunted me for the majority of my life abruptly stopped. My waking thoughts were now consumed by serious dangers to our security. Instead of feeling useless, I was encouraged as I sat up on the roof late at night thinking of ways to assist. Real problems must surely have real solutions.

As I informed Mamá, I was also sure that the countless hours I spent in church as an altar boy and in confession could be better spent working to aid the family. Furthermore, sitting in church was tedious, and my attention span was not my strongest asset. My mother paused for a bit before making her decision. "Alfredo, if you continue as you are until your First Communion, after that, it will be up to you to choose whether or not to attend church anymore."

She just had two requirements: one, I had to be observant and good during Easter week every year; and second, before receiving one Communion, I had to crawl into the sanctuary on my knees, confessing my sins as I crawled all the way to the altar.

Now I had to make a difficult choice. In my opinion, Easter was a dismal, sombre holiday. The rituals seemed bizarre to me, in contrast to my favourite holiday, Da de los Muertos, when we ate candy, danced, and dressed up in skeleton costumes and skull masks, paying homage to death while mocking its finality. Still, since these gestures meant so much to my mother and I just had to attend church once a year, this wasn't such a bad deal. The true problem would be being clean about my many transgressions in public.

And yet, at the age of ten, that's exactly what I did. On that lengthy crawl, as I shuffled on my knees up the steps and along the aisle on the cold, hard marble floor, I pleaded for forgiveness not just for past transgression but also for future wrongdoing. My faults were not generic or abstract; they were not terrible, but they were not insignificant. They featured the pyrotechnic experiments I'd carried out in the fields with my investigative team, in which we built flame geysers high in the air. As I had previously confessed to our priest, I had a history of not speaking the truth, the entire truth, and nothing but the truth when asked by my seniors. Though I didn't overtly lie, I had discovered a way to evade the truth by saying nothing, such as when I was seven or eight years old and my father questioned me about a particular brag I had made to the bigger guys in the schoolyard.

Rather of asking if I was serious when I said I could run around and pull up girls' dresses without them noticing, my father said, "Are you behaving yourself at school?""

I was furious. "Of course!" says one." This was true when we were talking about my behaviour in class, where I was an angel. A little devil got the better of me out in the yard.

"Tell me the truth, Alfredo, were you looking up girl's dresses?""

"What?" I put on a disgusted, shocked expression. I found that quite persuasive. "Who told you I did that?""

"Forget it. I'm curious whether you did or did not. Well?"

"And I say that's a terrible accusation, and whoever made it must have had no idea what they were talking about!""

We could go on for hours like this. I reasoned that as long as I wasn't caught in the act, I couldn't be convicted. But I felt deep down that my action was a sin by omission and promptly confessed to the priest. The priest appeared to be more concerned that I looked up girls' clothing than that I lied. Clearly, I wasn't living up to the church's moral standards or displaying the kind of character that respected my family and my parents' ideals.

I expressed genuine contrition for the incident while crawling on my knees outside the church. There was even more. Aside from possessing a sharp tongue and occasionally lashing out with scathing retorts, I was known to crack a dirty joke or two. Or even three.

I begged forgiveness for these and other sins all the way to the altar. Even though I had no cause to feel guilty for the gas station's demise, I requested forgiveness only in case anything I had done or not done had contributed to our tragedy. More importantly, I begged to be given the duty and strength to assist alleviate the issues, as well as the understanding to realise what was happening to us.

Thus, my association with organised religion came to an end. From then on, I communed with God wherever and whenever I wanted: at night under the stars, on my way to and from school, or on my way to various employment. My one-on-ones with God sometimes turned into passionate debates about why there was so much suffering, how could a merciful Supreme Being allow poverty, illness, injustice, and disaster to exist, and what had my innocent baby sister Maricela done to be removed from the world? Although the answers were fuzzy, my conviction that I will one day understand these mysteries was not.

Meanwhile, my mother was a source of inspiration for me in dealing with our earthly troubles. Mamá decided, unafraid and without complaint, that she was going to keep her family together, despite my parents' already fragile relationship and our recurring problems that had no easy solution.

Flavia, who was already resourceful, extended her activities. She immediately opened a small secondhand shop in a market area outside Palaco, in addition to buying and finding old products to renovate and sell. Her shop, located forty miles south of the border barrier that ran between Mexicali on the Mexican side and Calexico on the US side, drew both locals and visitors who wished to venture into the country but not too far. Mamá got an ancient sewing machine with a foot pedal and began doing piecework for a costume company at home at night-sewing, of all things, sexy clothes for hookers at the local brothel!

The community became aware of this particular piece, and I was not amused when the taunting began. Too bad for the child who scoffed at me one day, "What's it like to be the son of a prostitute's tailor?""

"What's it like to be the son of the woman she's making the clothes for?" I asked, using my harsh tongue."

After getting my buttocks kicked for making that statement, I was determined to fight less and find a better way to channel my outspoken personality. I started a hot dog stand with support from my Uncle Abel, one of my mother's brothers, and money from selling all the marbles I'd been collecting for years. Who could resist a child with a big voice selling hot dogs while standing on a stool? No one, I reasoned. Unfortunately, not everyone could afford my wares. I subsequently began selling roasted maize, but as the national economy deteriorated, I fared no better.

Desperation took hold. My mother's oldest brother, Uncle Jose, began to make occasional deliveries from the United States, where he worked and lived part-time, bringing food essentials and sometimes money that ensured we could feed for the next several months just as things were getting desperate. The sight of his pickup truck approaching us and kicking up dust on the road, loaded with burlap bags of beans, rice, and potatoes, reminded me of the arrival of the cavalry in old Western movies. We arrived just in time!

Uncle Jose's generosity was unknown to me at the time-he had few resources himself-but I knew he cared enough to help. Nobody ever told Uncle Jose how bad things had gotten for us. He found it out somehow.

No one else did, not even my mother's brother, Fausto, who travelled down from the United States every Christmas and brought my cousins, Fausto Jr. and Oscar, with him. Uncle Fausto had come to California as a migrant labourer in the 1950s using the Bracero Program's seasonal passports. He had found a permanent job as a senior foreman at a massive ranch in the hamlet of Mendota in the San Joaquin Valley, where he was raising his two sons as a divorced parent.

Uncle Fausto, a straightforward man, would have commented on our deteriorating circumstances if he had seen them. Instead, my mother had to bring it up and inquire about the prospect of coming to the United States for migrant work for the summer. Mamá originally mentioned the idea to my father, and he didn't object, though I assume he wasn't thrilled about the notion of having to travel across the border to America to harvest cotton and tomatoes. My mother decided to talk to Uncle Fausto on his yearly Christmas visit because he didn't have any other ideas.

This choice was made after months of conflict in our home. Nobody told us kids about it, but the look on my mother's face when my father arrived home in the middle of the night said it all. Papá never hit Mamá, but he had a loud voice, and when the two of them started arguing, the sound of his discontent filled our house, making me feel as if I couldn't breathe, much alone stopping them. Rosa got caught in the crossfire one day while Gabriel and I were in the background during a heated conversation. She stood between my parents, sobbing and pleading with them to stop yelling at each other.

Mamá realized we couldn't continue as we were. When she spoke to Uncle Fausto, however, her tone was casual, as she reminded him that we all had the necessary paperwork to travel back and forth across the border for tourism, so no new or special documentation was required. My mother proposed that she and my father work while the rest of us kids had a summer vacation.

"Let me see what I can do," Uncle Fausto shrugged.

We found out not long after that everything was set up for the summer and that when school let out, we were heading to Mendota for two months. Trip via car! I couldn't wait any longer. My trip to America was about to begin.

Mendota, California, bills itself as the cantaloupe centre of the world, which made me feel right at home because I grew up in melon country. But something else added familiarity to our trek, creating a literal link to my backyard at home. The Southern Pacific Railroad established Mendota in the late 1800s as a switching station and storage area for repairing and sheltering railroad cars, and most of California agriculture's products were emptied and reloaded here. What were the chances? The tracks that ran through Mendota were built at the Port of Stockton (where I would ultimately work), where ships arrived to dump cargo onto railcars at the water's edge. After Mendota, trains could be routed east or west, or they could continue south to the line's end in, well, Palaco!

Back in 1979, when I was eleven years old, none of the dots had yet joined for me. But that summer, I felt a sense of destiny. Mendota was as close to heaven as I could imagine as my first introduction to the United States-a Garden of Eden about forty miles west of Fresno in the centre of the fertile San Joaquin Valley that spans for miles from Stockton down through the middle of the state, almost to Bakersfield.

California produces up to a quarter of all produce cultivated in the United States, with the majority of it grown in the San Joaquin Valley. I was delighted in the freedom of the first true vacation I could recall as soon as we arrived at the ranch where Uncle Fausto was a foreman. We could also eat for free! I gazed out over field after field, as far as the eye could see, rich in bountiful growth and product of every variety. There were rolling hills, wooded glens, irrigation canals, and meandering dirt trails all around me, all demanding to be explored. In addition, my cousins Fausto and Oscar were always eager to engage in the fun with me and my siblings.

Every morning, after the grownups had gone to the fields, the main goal of the day was to find out how to get to a mystical spot we called "Faraway," where you wouldn't know you'd arrived until you got there! If I wanted a break from our adventures, I went to the garage where tractors and farm equipment were maintained, where I offered my mechanical knowledge and talent in driving heavy vehicles. I also began cleaning workers' rooms at a nearby barracks. I was in high demand since my charges were lower than the competition's.

Unfortunately, the rival, a fifteen-year-old, arrived with his gang and pursued me. One of the guys pushed me down and twisted my arm so severely that I couldn't clean it. Clearly, the time had come to learn some authentic Kaliman self-defence tactics.

As a result, when we returned to Mexico, my first instinct was to enrol in boxing instruction at a gym in Mexicali. But, having bid farewell to the paradise of Faraway/Mendota, our family was soon pushed as thin as ever, and I recognized that I would have to devise my own self-improvement program. So I devised a daring strategy to transform the outdoors into an obstacle course for my self-designed training program. Aha! I'd race against my prior pace on my way to school or work, pushing myself faster each day, sometimes creating athletic moves that involved leaping over creeks and catapulting over fences-anything to squeeze out another ounce of energy.

This was the Kaliman strategy. According to the hero's origins, his DNA was not superhuman. He had simply trained himself to be as strong as fifty men, to levitate and practise telepathy and ESP, and to battle evil and injustice without ever taking a life. With the exception of sedative darts used to momentarily sedate evildoers and a dagger used exclusively as a tool, he needed no weapons to defeat an opponent. Kaliman would even put his own life in danger to prevent the death of another human being. He was also a scientist, regularly spouting amazing information about nature and the cosmos while embracing the achievement of knowledge with ideas such as "He who masters the mind masters everything." He was dressed fully in white save for the jewel-encrusted letter "K" on his turban.

Fortunately, even though I was the youngest student and the teacher's darling, school remained a great place for me to build on mental mastery. These anxieties grew as I transferred schools and lost my community of defenders. Worse, there were some quite frightening students at the school. Mauricio, a tower of muscle, did back flips and propelled off walls like a circus acrobat, and whenever he went by, the ground trembled. The only person who wasn't terrified of him was his sidekick, known as El Gallo because he crows like a rooster after he defeats everybody who was in his way. The Rooster was one of the tallest thirteen-year-olds I'd ever seen, with long, sinewy arms built for punches and uppercuts. These two were at the top of the list of youngsters I was trying to avoid as part of my survival strategy. What do you think? Mauricio was sitting just behind me in my natural science class, leaning over my shoulder to copy off my tests.

I only saw one solution: offer him and his fellow bad boys my tutoring services. We agreed on a charge in exchange for a guarantee that they would defend us from any larger thugs. They were on my payroll, as I previously stated.

My students did not benefit as much from the tutoring sessions as I had intended. Their underlying comprehension increased, but I quickly realised that the more expeditious (and profitable) way was to let them copy my answers on my examinations. Of course, I realised this was the wrong solution, and I didn't pretend otherwise. On the plus side, the school witnessed a decrease in misbehaviour during this time.

I could contribute to our family's well-being while also keeping up with my education through tutoring and restaurant jobs. However, I soon began to bemoan the fact that I couldn't have a social life outside of school. I'd had my fair share of flirtations with females in my class when I was fourteen, but I didn't have the money or time to pursue romance. There will be no dates, no dances, and no strolls down the street holding hands. Is it true that I felt sorry for myself? No, I couldn't accept that. But working every waking hour outside of school, day in and day out, was clearly becoming old.

I finally revealed my feelings to my mother, trying to explain for the millionth time why, at the age of fourteen, I believed that the time had come for me to return to Mendota for the summer, on my own. If I could work there for two months, I could aid the family so much more than if I stayed in Mexico. Moreover, I could put money away so that I wouldn't have to work full-time during the school year.

This would also help me to move more rapidly in completing the unique training program I'd recently begun that was the equivalent of a college curriculum for individuals preparing to become teachers. Mamá and Papá agreed that becoming an educator was a wonderful decision for me: not only was it a respectable career, but it would enable me to start earning a living in a shorter amount of time than, for instance, studying to become a lawyer or a doctor. And, in the greatest of all circumstances, if I become a teacher, I could afford to continue my studies toward those other professions if I wished.

Although I didn't have a work permit for my summer plans, that hurdle could be bypassed with the passports that enable us to go back and forth across the border. Nothing anyone could say was going to convince me that this survival plan was not a good idea; it was the only concept. Mamá finally succumbed and walked to the phone booth to dial Uncle Fausto's number.

"Absolutely not," dad said flatly when mom asked whether I could go back to Mendota and work in the fields for the summer. He soon added, however, that he would love for me to come for a holiday.

I was grateful for his offer and vowed to persuade him otherwise. I sat silently in the passenger seat of a car driven by a relative who was travelling that way for the entire ride up to Central California, pondering how to persuade Uncle Fausto to give me a chance to prove myself. When I was finally dropped off in front of my uncle's house, I gathered my courage and stood there with my few belongings under my arm, not sure what I could say would sway him. I could tell Uncle Fausto and my cousins were surprised when they came out to see me at 102 pounds, far skinnier than when my Mendota relatives had last seen me. "Are you hungry?" said Uncle Fausto right away."

Before I could respond, an ice cream truck with a swarm of dancing children came down the road, playing happy organ-grinder music. Uncle Fausto motioned toward the truck and inquired, "Would you like some ice cream?"" After warmly thanking him, I had the pleasure of tasting my first-ever rainbow-coloured, push-up sherbet. I was in ecstasy as I savoured its creamy, sweet delectability. And it was a small tidbit in comparison to Uncle Fausto's big dinner that evening. I thought I could easily forget about work for the next two months and just enjoy life. But as soon as I thought that, a picture of my family in Mexico came to mind, sitting around the table every night and subsisting on the most modest food.

That night, I launched my campaign with Uncle Fausto, assuring him how valuable I would be in the fields. He flatly refused once more. After some back and forth, my uncle said, "Okay, give me five good reasons why I should give you a job."

I don't recall the first four, but I do recall the last: I looked Uncle Fausto in the eyes and replied, "Because we need it at home."

He looked at me intently and said nothing. He finally nodded his head. "Fine," responded the man, "if you're ready to go at five A.M., I'll put you to work."

I waited outside Uncle Fausto's truck fifteen minutes early the next morning, ready to prove myself. There was no particular treatment. I was dropped off with a predominantly male workforce and began at the bottom of the migrant-worker ladder, pulling weeds. By the conclusion of my two months, I had progressed from pulling weeds in cotton and tomato fields to picking and carting crops, working with sorting and counting equipment, and eventually taking over one of the coveted tractor-driving positions.

During breaks, I remained to myself, reading a book I'd taken with me to keep up my studies and fuel my mind so that I could focus on the physical obstacles of work rather than being overwhelmed by mundane or tough chores. I was proud that I could work harder than anyone else, not because of a difference in abilities, but because of the sense of urgency that drove me-the strong sense of purpose that came from knowing that every penny earned would put food on the table for my parents and siblings and allow me to help improve my family's situation.

When I did go out at night with my cousins and uncle, the primary topic of conversation was boxing. And it was in this setting that I was given the nickname "Doc," possibly as a foreshadowing of things to come. But, for many years, there was no medical relationship.

People in Mexican culture are frequently given more than one nickname; we may have several that are only distantly related to one another. When I originally came to Mendota with my family, most of my nicknames were Americanized variations of Alfredo, ranging from Freddy to Alfred, Fred, and Fredo. When I was fourteen, I was introduced to Rocky, the quintessential underdog, and was bestowed with a slew of new nicknames. My uncle dubbed me "Ferdie" in honour of Dr. Ferdie Pacheco, the famed boxing medic who had been Muhammad Ali's beloved cornerman and personal doctor. Then he and my cousins began referring to me as Dr. Pacheco, which evolved into "Doctor" and, finally, just "Doc."

Everyone in the field assumed that when they heard my family refer to me as Doc or Dr. Pacheco, it explained why I studied so much and was so serious and thorough in everything I did—as if each assignment were a matter of life and death. Some of them thought I was a doctor!

Looking back, I realise that much of my ferocity arose from my lingering disappointment that my family's position had not changed. No doubt, some of my rage was directed at my father, because so much had fallen on my mother's shoulders. He blamed himself for the loss of the gas station, but I thought it was time for him to move on after five years. Nonetheless, he was trapped. But the struggle I was fighting against a growing sense of hopelessness was much more strong than the fury. I realised the only way to deal with it was to work myself to the bone and squeeze every last cent out of every second. I had reduced to 92 pounds after two months of this strict diet and refusing to spend any of my wages. My normally round face had been drawn, with sunken cheeks, and I needed to punch three holes in my belt to keep my pants up.

Uncle Fausto often reminded me that I needed new clothes. Finally, he stated that we were going shopping on my last Sunday in Mendota, whether I liked it or not. "Okay, Dr. Pacheco," he began as my cousins and I entered the men's and boys' clothing store, which carried a variety of prominent brands, "buy yourself a new wardrobe."

I stood there transfixed, refusing to even look at the clothes, let alone spend a penny of what I'd earned. But how could I defy my uncle, whose generosity had enabled me to thrive?

When Uncle Fausto saw my paralysis, he shrugged and continued to select out two pairs of jeans and two shirts in my size that he knew I'd enjoy, before heading for the cash register. When I pointed out that such products could be purchased for less money in Mexico, he didn't seem to care. "Doc," he said, "give me your wallet."

"No," I said flatly.

"Freddy, give me your wallet."

My eyes welled up with tears. My cousins averted their gaze. Finally, I caved and took the money, just over $50, and paid for the apparel that I really needed and secretly desired.

On that shopping trip, Uncle Fausto taught me an important lesson. He wanted me to understand that taking care of oneself was not selfish, and that while sharing the fruits of my labour with others was great, hard work should also result in some personal rewards. To emphasise that point, the next day, as he and my cousins drove me to the Greyhound station, just before I boarded the bus, Uncle Fausto surprised me with a present of his Walkman, complete with recordings of American rock and roll. He'd seen me at the store pricing tape players and knew how desperately I wanted one. It was one of the most thoughtful gifts I'd ever received.

One of the few gifts that came close came within a day of my return home. Mamá burst into tears the instant she saw me-92 pounds of skin and bones-as I stepped off the bus in Mexicali. But I assured her that I had something for her that would make her happy. When we got home, just the two of us in the kitchen, I reached into my right sock, under the ball of my foot, and pulled out the roll of banknotes I had guarded with every atom of my might on the bus ride back to Mexico. Approximately fifty dollars less than a thousand dollars. The look of surprise and relief on my mother's face when I handed her the money-enough to feed us for a year and save for the future-was the best personal reward I could have received.

My mother ultimately persuaded me to buy a set of old boxing gloves after I had been back from Mendota for about a year, so that I could fulfil my ambition of working out at a gym in Mexicali. I'd regained the weight I'd lost by then, and I was soon working my way up to lightweight status at 130 pounds. I admit that I was weary of getting my butt kicked, being a target, and having to surround myself with bigger guys for safety. A part of me also fantasised about exacting vengeance on a particular punk who had insulted me many years before. To my regret, I later utilised my boxing talents outside the ring to call him out on the street and brutally beat him-a wrong that would haunt me for years. I'd then discover the reality of Kaliman's concept, "Revenge is a poor counsellor."

But as I pummelling the punching bag, all I could think about was how life had been knocking us down and how I needed to find a new way to respond. My time as a boxer taught me that I could do more than bob and weave defensively in the face of a threat; my training taught me to fight back and, when required, to be the aggressor. This conclusion was quickly reinforced by the first two of my three ring fights, which I won. But I wasn't so sure in the third and last battle, when I encountered a physically strong opponent who left me to taste my own blood-especially when he knocked me to my knees just before the bell in the final round. Still, I had a choice: quit or stand up and battle on, even if I was defeated. By opting for the latter, I learnt a vital lesson: defeat should not be feared; more important than whether I won or lost was how I responded to being pushed down and thrown off balance.

Though this was my final official fight, boxing had provided me with what I needed at the time-a chance to retaliate. I also realised that, similar to the corner breaks that allowed me to recharge during battles, there were other ways to recharge my batteries. Eye-opening!

But I still had a lot of rage because I needed someone to blame for the disasters that had been going on for far too long. Rather than fighting in the ring, I began reserving my rage and revolt for the forces, institutions, and authority that most dominated my life. The biggest unfairness that ate at me at the time was my country's continual split of social classes, which devalued human beings in the lowest economic strata, as if only those at the top with political connections, wealth, and means were deserving of respect and opportunity. Part of my battle was to keep those values from affecting me.

My grandparents were always a guiding light for how to respond positively to adversity. They were both growing up in years and fighting terrible ailments. Though I knew in theory that they wouldn't be there forever, Tata Juan and Nana Maria had always seemed larger than life, and I couldn't imagine losing them.

On a typical day, one of my cousins arrived in my school's director's office to request that I be excused from class, explaining that my grandfather, who was dying of metastatic lung cancer, had called for me. We drove to my grandparents' house, and I felt I was too late as I rushed into Tata's chamber. He appeared to be staring off beyond space, having already left in spirit. When I approached him, I noticed that his eyelids were closed.

"Tata," I whispered into his ear, reaching in close with one hand on his shoulder and the other on the aged skin of his cheek. "It's me, Alfredo."

"Oh, yes," he said laboriously. "Alfredo."

My tears started falling helplessly. I had seen him frequently in recent months, as cancer was slowly and horribly killing him, but I had rarely persuaded him to talk much. I wasn't ready to say goodbye despite seeing him decline.

The sound of his breathing and the ticking of a little clock on his bedside were unforgettable in the otherwise silent room. Then my grandfather opened his eyes slowly and softly and asked, "Do you remember when we used to go to the Rumorosa Mountains?"

"Yes, I do. Always."

"Me too. 'Tataaaahhhh! Tataaaahhhh!' you used to say."

"I remember."

"You know," he added as he closed his eyes and smiled goodbye, "I really enjoyed those times."

Tata's last words reassured me that I should not be scared to climb mountains, no matter how dangerous they were, and that I could even enjoy it. He wasn't telling me how to do it, but he did want me to know that I could keep calling on him whenever I felt lost.

After Nana Maria died two years later, I felt her presence with me as well-though her lesson was to be cautious and watch for pitfalls. I hope she forgives me for not being by her side more during her final days. Nana went to the grave knowing that no one had died in her care after a career as a healer, assisting in the birth of hundreds of lives. But I was astonished to learn from my father that she was terrified of dying till the end, particularly the loneliness of not knowing what lay on the other side. My father also told me that, despite her worry, she would be ready when the time came. Nana understood what many of us will never know until we are there: no matter how many times we overcome the odds, we all reach a point where surrender is the only option. What about now? Give it your all!

Christmas 1985 was memorable for several reasons. At seventeen, almost eighteen, I was on my way to become one of the youngest students ever to graduate from the training program at the teaching college that would serve as my springboard into the future. After graduating with outstanding grades and teacher references, I would wait to see where I would be posted in Mexico to begin my career as an elementary school teacher. At the time, I also had a wonderful girlfriend, a lovely, brilliant young lady from a well-to-do, well-respected family. Our courting was new, but we were both committed to our futures enough to pursue a lasting relationship.

After many problems, I was optimistic that better days were ahead, as I told my cousin Fausto and his friend Ronnie as they drove down from Mendota for the Christmas vacation in Fausto's truck. My objective, I told them, was to secure a lucrative assignment for my first teaching job, ideally in one of the larger cities nearer to home. The government occasionally assigned newer instructors who lacked the necessary family connections to remote places where there was little money to be made and few opportunities for additional education. But, given my stellar academic record, I anticipated to be rewarded with the right job.

We decided to go to Mexicali to attend a holiday party with some of my friends. We had wheels and could set the scene in style thanks to Fausto's vehicle, which was a significant plus for me given that I generally had to take the bus to such locations and then walk three kilometres or more in great heat or cold. We were so mobile, in fact, that Fausto and Ronnie proposed we carry on to additional parties over the border in Calexico, California, not long after we arrived at the Mexicali party.

It's a little issue. I didn't have my passport with me. I'd left it at home because I hadn't intended to cross the border. Fausto offered to drive us back to my place for it, but I couldn't see the point of driving two hours for a piece of paper. The party would be over by the time we accomplished that. "Never mind," I said to Fausto, "I'm not going to need it." They rarely stop us."

We neared the border crossing checkpoint. The agent, who appeared to be in a festive mood, began to wave us through when something caught his eye and he motioned for us to stop.

The American agent, who was standing by the driver's side, asked Fausto in English where he was going. Fausto explained that he was from Fresno but was visiting family for the holidays and was only crossing the border for a party.

The representative nodded. "Where are you from?" he asked Ronnie.

Ronnie replied, "Fresno." He was taken at his word by the agent.

To escape further queries, I claimed to be looking at something beyond the window, high in the sky. "You!" the agent exclaimed. "Where do you come from?"

"Fresno," I said, echoing Fausto and Ronnie's tone and accent. In this era, I knew almost little about the English language.

"And how long have you lived in Fresno, son?" said the border agent.

"Fresno," I said, nodding and smiling.

The agent then requested documentation, which I, of course, did not have.

A swarm of agents surrounded the truck in seconds. They let Fausto and Ronnie go but kept me after much deliberation. Following a two-hour interrogation, I constantly protested that I had just misplaced my passport and meant no harm or crime. I knew I couldn't give them my name since it would result in the permanent suspension of my passport. I couldn't tell them what I did or where I came from either. But I couldn't tell a lie.

The border official who stopped us, who spoke Spanish, requested blood. He could tell I was naked because I was dressed in lightweight shorts, a tank top, and flip-flops. He started threatening my loved ones, despite the fact that he had no idea who they were. He put me in a terribly chilly chamber that was as near to a cell as I would ever come. I wept myself to sleep, curled up in a foetal posture in a vain attempt to get warm, convinced that my life was over.

Another agent arrived before daybreak to unlock the door and discovered me on the floor. He was a caring man who was plainly furious with the other agents for keeping me in such deplorable conditions for so long without food or water. The agent apologised, gave me money for breakfast, and waved me off.

The lesson has been learned. My better judgement was definitely tainted. It was terrible enough that I didn't have a plan in case I was stopped. But by believing I could fool the border patrol official who first approached the automobile, I crossed the line between confidence and arrogance. With regret, I decided never to travel again without my passport.

I wasn't sure I wanted to travel again after that ordeal. But mitigating circumstances shifted my perspective. To my surprise, as soon as I graduated from college, I discovered that, due to the political climate in Mexico, my academic credentials had not helped me get the job I desired. Instead, I was to begin working immediately in a remote, rural place. Better jobs in cities near colleges had all gone to students from more affluent and politically connected families. How could the fight have been so obviously rigged? What about the concept of merit? What about talent and perseverance? What about fairness and equality?

Without realising it, I was already putting into practice what I'd learned about the American ideal during my two excursions to the San Joaquin Valley, at the ages of eleven and fourteen. I wanted to believe that I could travel to Faraway in my own country and have adventures while still meeting opportunity and success. I wanted to believe that, like my hero, Benito Juárez, I could appear out of nowhere and make significant contributions to my country. I desperately wanted to believe that people like me, who are poor and politically marginalised, are not powerless. For a decade, economic difficulties intensified poverty and suffering, leaving the once-thriving middle class in the dust. Now I was learning that the promise that had kept me going-that people like me who had plummeted to the bottom could someday change our own circumstances-was a fairytale.

My future was now in jeopardy. Is it true that I wanted to be an elementary school teacher? Had I truly excelled, or did learning come naturally to me? As I reflected on my recent years of study, I realised that I'd had little passion for my subject matter and now, more than ever, detested this system for luring me in with promises it couldn't keep. Had I chosen my path because it was feasible, or because someone else had done it and left a trail for me? Had I given up on the dreams that had fueled my battling spirit since I was a child?

Everything felt more difficult than before, and my condition appeared bleak at times. At times, I wondered if my life was worth living, if anyone would mourn me if I died. Yes, I had a supportive family and a partner who thought I had something to give. But they could have been mistaken. Maybe everyone would be better off if I didn't exist.

Nobody could convince me that I was probably suffering from a long-overdue episode of despair or that my disenchantment was age-appropriate. Nobody told me that this sad era would help me in the future by allowing me to empathise with patients and comprehend their hardships.

One image saved me from despair: the memory of my mother's joyous expression when I returned from Mendota and handed her my cash. That hard-earned money demonstrated that individuals like me were not powerless or helpless. That was valuable, I had to acknowledge. I also found solace in a dream that came to me during this period of near despair. In it, a shadowy stranger informed me that better days were ahead and that I could shape my own destiny, but I would have to leave everything familiar behind to do so. I inquired of the stranger how I would know if I was on the correct track. He said a woman with fair hair and green eyes will arrive to accompany me at the appropriate stage of the journey.

Other than that, the dream was vague. However, remembering my mother's expression when I arrived home from working in the fields the last time, I concluded I could still become a teacher if I made a few changes to my plan. If I returned to Mendota for a short time, I could save enough money to buy a car and supplement my poor income when I returned to Mexico to begin my community service position. Uncle Fausto graciously agreed to reinstate me at the ranch, where I relished my recovered title of Dr. Pacheco. I quickly accumulated $700 in wages and needed no convincing to purchase a wreck of an old Thunderbird from a nearby used-car business.

My fantasy of transforming the car's interior into a Las Vegas attraction-complete with images of movie stars, dice, religious imagery, and a cassette player to blast the heavy rock I'd discovered- would have to be put on hold. But, in the interim, that Thunderbird crash travelled much further and back than its designers could have dreamed.

3. The Kaliman Maneuver

How did I manage it?

Even now, I'm not sure how I managed to get over the border and start a new life in California. In the years since, I've frequently stated that I was motivated by a combination of bravado and inexperience. Why else would I defy gravity and risk injuring, imprisoning, or even dying to cross the border? It would have been far more difficult to screen out damaging thoughts if there had been some degree of ignorance about all the things that could go wrong. If I had been more realistic and carefully weighed the risks, I might not have gone on the trip at all.

But I wasn't completely unaware of the risk I was taking on that New Year's Day in 1987. I was fully conscious that the approach I'd devised over the night would fail as I watched the sun rise over the fields of home for probably the last time. Life has taught me to be fearless in the face of failure. What made me more terrified was not attempting to grasp the world that was just out of reach. My fear was that I would not go for it, that I would not give it my all. And it wasn't for lack of chutzpah or lack of worldly experience. It stemmed from the conviction that I possessed valuable qualities to offer—my passion (Quinones tenacity) and inexhaustible energy, even if I didn't yet know how to channel it in a useful way.

These resources were also useful in my strategy for crossing the border without papers. Desperation undoubtedly poured gasoline to the fire. But the scientist within me was already hard at work. Remembering Tata Juan's words, I knew that I needed to deviate from the well-beaten route in order to construct a good future. And, anticipating the counsel of the renowned scientist Santiago Ramón y Cajal, whose writing would have a significant impact on my career, I instinctively realised that I needed to think clearly, prepare my strategy thoroughly, and never give up. Of course, having just put my school books away to prepare for full-time employment on the lowest rungs of agriculture, I would have scoffed at the idea of becoming a scientist, let alone a neuroscientist, one day.

My plan was not flawless. As any scientist could have told me, most great discoveries are the result of trial and error, repetition and adaptation, imaginative leaps, and the all-important commodity of good luck, which we are not permitted to admit in the scientific world.

Indeed, there was nothing scientific about my decision to violate the prevailing opinion that the safest way to cross without being apprehended by border police was to cut a hole in the fence or tunnel beneath it. According to legend, if not the truth, persons who attempted to scale the barrier, as I planned to do, and then were entangled in the barbed wire suffered the most severe injuries, and some even perished. Although armed vigilantes were not common at the time, the majority of stories regarding border gunshot deaths concerned persons attempting to cross over rather than under the fence.

Perhaps it was the underdog in me—the boy who was used to being challenged and who wanted to do things differently—that chose the risky path. And, being a rebellious soul, I saw no appeal in taking the easy route—or so I attempted to explain to Gabriel, Fausto, and Oscar on the evening of January 1, as the sun began to set during our journey to the drop-off site in Mexicali.

"Doc, you're crazy!" mocked cousin Oscar from the rear seat of my Thunderbird, next to Gabriel. "Nobody jumps the fence." Nobody jumped the barrier in the middle of Calexico, he meant but didn't have to tell. In fact, many people discovered remote portions of the fence to climb. However, attempting to do it in the centre of town was insane.

I looked across at Fausto, who was driving, from the front passenger seat. "Well, I think we're using the word 'jump' as a euphemism, right Freddy?" asked Fausto, in his gentle, knowledgeable manner.

"Exactly." Then I explained that my manoeuvre would be more of a Spiderman climb up the eighteen-foot fence, followed by a hop over the barbed wire and a leap toward foreign soil-culminating in a flying descent and a pantherlink, spring-loaded landing, similar to the Kaliman manoeuvre that I'd never mastered.

Despite Oscar and Gabriel's reservations about this ridiculous scheme, we were all psyched by the prospect of the adventure.

For all of the danger that the gravity-defying section of the crossing entailed, the rest of the plan was gentler and had fewer potential dangers. So I insisted, telling Fausto to pull over a few blocks from the border fence where I planned to attempt "the manoeuvre."

Fausto would then drive the three miles or so west to the major crossing gate where cars entered the United States from Mexico, and then slowly make his way through the streets of Calexico to our predetermined meeting point behind the house of one of our relatives. When I landed on the other side of the fence, my plan was to take off in the opposite direction of the Thunderbird, spend some time in order to miss the trail of any suspicious border officers, and finally return to our place. After we got out of town and onto the highway, the story thickened as we implemented a few techniques to dodge the immigration checkpoints, which were actually the most difficult part of most border crossings.

With the various advances in technology, many more inspections along numerous transit lines, and considerably harsher measures at the US-Mexico border, this concept of mine would no longer work- and for good reason. Immigration issues have become considerably more difficult, and we still have a long way to go in figuring out how to achieve fair-minded change while taking all of these factors into account.

In some ways, however, things have increased rather than changed, including economic extremes in both developing and industrialised countries. Literal hunger and a desire for opportunity are enough to drive the poor and helpless to risk everything, including their lives, to cross the border. Meanwhile, anti-immigrant sentiment has intensified, primarily toward poor, illegal labourers who supply cheap labour.

As I would subsequently discover, industrialised countries will always welcome the Einsteins of the world-those individuals whose abilities have already been recognized and deemed valuable. This welcome is typically not extended to impoverished and uneducated people wishing to enter the country. The truth, however, is that the most entrepreneurial, innovative, and motivated citizen is the one who has been given an opportunity and wants to repay the debt. This is confirmed by historical facts and the richness of the immigrant contribution to America's distinction in the world.

Of course, I had no idea these intricacies existed as I prepared to cross the border. The fence stood between oppression and a fighting chance for me, between stagnation and hope. It was that easy. Furthermore, the United States was experiencing unprecedented demand for trustworthy cheap labour-decent, hardworking, and capable. This indicated to me that I was required. My drama was set on this stage.

It was make-or-break time at 8:30 p.m. I approached the border barrier, which was a few blocks beyond Mexicali's city boundaries. I was relieved to find that I cast very little shadow as I crouched next to a shrub between two light towers. I was aware, however, that as I got closer to the barrier, I would be clearly visible to anyone in the area. Even though there were no motion detectors at the time, one false move, one flinch of a muscle, could cause the project to fail.

Gabriel and Oscar were a few hundred yards behind me, hiding behind a tree in the darkness, observing my attempt to make history-to accomplish something none of us had ever considered or witnessed before. I imagined that the lights would allow them to see not just me scale the fence, but also to gaze across to the area in Calexico where Fausto would pick me up. I assumed their difficulty would be to hide their cheers as the Thunderbird flew away—and to avoid any other noise or movement that would catch the attention of the Mexican police who monitored the border on our side.

At 8:31 p.m., I take the moment, fill my lungs with air, and knowing that my brother and younger cousin were watching, muster every ounce of guts and showmanship I could generate to propel myself over the fence and pull out all the Kaliman stops. Even though Gabriel and Oscar were rooting for me to cross the fence safely and effortlessly, I knew they would be just as happy to see me fall. Oh, ye of little faith, I thought as it dawned on me that I was actually doing this. In an instant, I realised what all those years of agility training had been preparing me for. I jumped into the air and vaulted over the top rolls of barbed wire with a jump, hop, and a leap, putting my body the proper distance from the fence and gliding down through the starless winter night with the grace of a bird. I was completely excited when I landed gracefully on my feet. Yes, yes, yes, I did it! The eagle had arrived. I had completed the manoeuvre! Just a minor hiccup. Based on my scientific calculations, I determined that I needed three minutes to cross the border before rushing away on foot into Calexico's streets. My estimations, however, were thirty seconds off. Headlights flashed into the darkness, briefly blinding me—amid the screaming of brakes and the churning of dust as the two border patrol officials threw open the automobile doors and immediately appeared on either side of me.

So much for pulling off the trick. I was humiliated and felt like a terrible loser. I imagined my brother and cousin rolling around on the ground, laughing uncontrollably. Despite my bold, scientific, and visionary thinking, the fireworks had just gone off. What happens next? Morosely, I braced myself to be branded not only a threat, but also an incompetent one. To my amazement, the border agents were a pleasant couple. In fact, my arrest was as ordinary and innocuous as they come in the annals of law enforcement.

I was then driven back to the main crossing station in a military-style Ford Bronco and ushered into a booking area. When asked, I offered the agents a fictitious name, thinking they wouldn't press the subject. I was a thin, defeated-looking teen who appeared to be sixteen and lacked even facial hair. They had nothing to gain by thrusting my defeat in my face. Without saying anything, the officials seemed empathetic, as if they understood the kinds of hardships that had motivated me to risk life and limb to cross the border without papers. But everyone has a task to complete. And they did what they always do: they kicked me back to Mexico, out the back door, to walk home.

I remember doing some real soul searching as I plodded down the three miles in the direction of my unsuccessful border crossing—where I'd last seen Gabriel and cousin Oscar. I was devastated. How might the path of last resort lead to nowhere? But then I wondered if it was just my ego that was injured. In my thoughts, I re-entered the ring and resolved to be my own cornerman, to summon both the Dr. Ferdie Pacheco and the Ali within me. I was certainly knocked down. My timing was, indeed, incorrect. But was I going to break down and cry? No way. I was going to retaliate and give it my all again, this time with a revised plan and new calculations.

I rushed toward the crossing place, excited to show my brother and cousin my new strategy. I figured they'd been watching the whole thing and couldn't wait to see me eat crow.

But when they watched me fly into the darkness, they had no idea what had happened. While I was being booked, Gabriel and Oscar were being booked by two Mexican cops who had picked them up simply because they looked suspicious, hiding behind a tree for no apparent reason and looking young and naive—one of them (cousin Oscar) well dressed in U.S.-bought clothes. They had never been in trouble before, so they believed things couldn't get any worse when the officers put them in the police cruiser. However, after a few minutes of driving, the officer in the passenger seat turned around and discovered a nearly empty bottle of beer at Oscar's feet.

As he turned to his colleague, the officer behind the wheel was furious. "We just got these kids in the car, and they're drinking?"

Gabriel and Oscar were hauled into the station and quickly escorted to a detention cell, where they delved into their pockets. Gabriel barely had a few dollars to spend. But Oscar ended up paying something exorbitant—say, a hundred dollars.

That scenario was still unfolding for them when I returned to where I had attempted my over-the-fence manoeuvre an hour before. I had no idea what to do next. All I knew was that I was lucky because I had a choice: throw in the towel and give up, or get back on my feet and try again, like I had learned in boxing. This decision put my mettle to the test, and it taught me a lesson that I've carried with me ever since: the best triumphs frequently come after numerous failures; the key is to try again and again without losing passion or focus.

When given the option, I chose to go for it again-the same plan, but better. To that goal, I spent the following hour hugging the ground next to the fence, beneath a few shrubs, and observing the border patrol's activities. Instead of allowing myself three minutes, I would have to reduce my actions into two minutes and thirty seconds. I'd moved too quickly on my initial attempt, and the agents had seen me in their patrol car's rear-view mirror.

Some would have thought it foolish to repeat the same move that had led to my capture the first time. It made great sense to me. The border officers would not expect me to return in a few hours and try the same thing that had failed before. Who would be that insane, you think? They must have reasoned that lightning would not strike twice in the same area. I should have known better!

So, once again, in a matter of seconds, I rose to the top of the fence and soared over it to the other side. My flight was much less graceful this time, as I came dangerously close to becoming entangled in the barbed wire at the top of the fence, then bit the dust and crashed to a less-than-comfortable landing. But before I'd even set foot on the ground, I was sprinting so quickly that my feet cut through the air, the motion of my legs propelling me as rapidly as the wind. With my heart pounding in my chest, I moved so quickly that I nearly fell again, nearly collapsing to the ground. Instead, I sped into alleys, over more gates, beneath laundry-draped clotheslines, and over fields, rousing a fierce pack of dogs that barked in unison as they chased me through the city. Finally, I arrived in the area where Fausto was supposed to meet me. When I turned the last curve, there he was, waiting in the darkness in my Thunderbird.

He came carefully, reaching across to open the door, and I jumped inside the car while it was still moving. We high-fived as I gathered my breath, neither of us saying anything, and he drove us away from the border, along Calexico's well-lit main street, until we blended in with all the automobiles driven by local revellers continuing their New Year's Eve festivities from the night before. We then turned west and circled until we arrived at the route heading to San Diego, which mercifully had no checks.

The strategy's second phase required Fausto to drop me off at the San Diego airport. The plot became much more complicated at this point, with the ending relying less on science and more on luck. I'd read that some people paid smugglers $600 to coordinate and carry out such a plot, but with only $65 to my name, I was forced to design my own improvised version.

I was on pins and needles, not knowing what to expect. I'd been on an adrenaline high since my passport was taken, receiving barely a few hours of sleep here and there. By now, exhaustion should have set in. There is no way! My heart rate increased as Fausto and I discussed the next steps. To bypass the Indio checkpoint, we had to split in San Diego and then reconnect in Los Angeles, most likely in the early morning. Prior to 9/11, airport security and ID requirements were not as strict for short local flights as they were for transcontinental and international travel.

My big bet was that I'd be able to buy a ticket and board an aircraft for the short flight to L.A. (and so bypass the checkpoints along Fausto's path) without having to show my ID. But, of course, this wasn't a novel notion, and ticket agents would have been on the watch for folks like me. So, on the drive to the airport, Fausto had assisted me in memorising and practising responses to some of the questions I would be asked. I practised my best American accent by listening to his pronunciation of important phrases-"A ticket to Los Angeles, please"-and then repeating them.

Only when Fausto dropped me off at the San Diego airport in the middle of the night and raced away into the darkness did I feel truly terrified. I began to panic as I waited in line at the airport ticket booth, fearful that immigration officers would emerge and surround me. Despite my trendy American Bugle Boy pants and posh Le Tigre polo shirt, I didn't think my outfit fooled anyone.

When my turn came, I approached the woman at the airline desk, worried that my heart would burst out of my chest. I drew on every memory I could find of earlier accomplishments in conquering my fears: driving a car for the first time at the age of five, overcoming stage fright at my first public speaking engagement, and transforming scary bullies into bodyguards. These ideas calmed my anxiety, and I added, with as much charm as I could muster, "A ticket to L.A., please."

"Next flight out, sir?"

"Yes, thank you." I almost said "my lady" like Tata Juan and placed a slight doff of my imaginary hat in there.

The ticket cost sixty-three bucks and change.

I paid for it and nodded gratefully, carefully tucking away the remaining dollar and coins and glancing around to see where I should go next. I had no other choice but to follow the early-morning crowd, which led me to the plane's departure location. The flight was incredible, amazing, and stomach-churning. No one in authority ever asked for my identification or questioned me. Despite this, I didn't breathe until we touched down in Los Angeles and drew up to the gate.

But the scheme has now lost all scientific control. Fausto had merely stated that he would do his best to meet me when I disembarked because he had no idea what plane or airline I would be on. If I didn't see him when I stepped off the plane, the plan was for me to wait for him in the lower level of the terminal entry beside the baggage carousel-despite the fact that we had no knowledge the airport had many terminals. So I wasn't concerned when he didn't appear at the gate to greet the plane, or when a few hours passed and he hadn't appeared at the terminal entry where I'd arrived. Though I was apprehensive, I assumed he had returned to Mexicali to retrieve Oscar and would eventually appear.

While the previous two days had sped by, the hours had now slowed to a halt. Of course, I wanted to run victory laps around LAX, but I wouldn't be able to relax until we were on our way to the San Joaquin Valley. Besides, I was starving, even after spending my last dollar and a half on a cheeseburger in the first place I came across-Burger King. I opted to tour the airport instead of worrying about where Fausto was and spent the rest of the day listening to the great assortment of talks, languages, and dialects. I went to the food court at one point, weak from hunger, expecting to find leftovers at other tables. I saw a couple with two children rush off to catch their flight, leaving their trays behind. I moved over to bus the table with the dexterity of a gazelle, surreptitiously munching on the food that would have gone to waste otherwise.

The food boosted my energy and enthusiasm, but by late afternoon, I was agitated, ready to give up hope that Fausto and I would ever meet. The prospect of having to fend for myself became all too real. True, I knew no one in Los Angeles, had little money, and could barely communicate in English. But if my path had led me here, I would have followed it into the city, where someone would acknowledge my hard work and hire me to sweep floors or pump petrol. And just as I resigned myself to this fate, as I stepped onto the down escalator-in a terminal distant from where I arrived-to make my way into the chill of the evening, Fausto appeared on the other side of the escalator! Unbelievable! What were the chances? We could have circled the airport for days and never found each other. But then he appeared! I'll never forget the look on his face and his warm smile as he looked up at me.

We hopped into my Thunderbird and drove out of the parking lot into the cool night air of Los Angeles, California. We swerved off and away, onto the freeway, following the signs north, before I could get a sense of the city. I finally allowed myself to yell and holler once we were out of town, and to thank the saints above for the miracle of this opportunity. All of this happened on January 2, 1987, my eighteenth birthday, if memory serves.

4. Lessons from the Fields

Winter is frequently the most difficult season for year-round migrant workers. This harsh reality was revealed to me shortly after my return to the San Joaquin Valley, along with a slew of other eye-opening revelations regarding the new route I had chosen. Aside from the chilly, wet weather that met me upon arrival, the year-round work cycle was considerably different from the brief stints I'd previously done at the ranch. Seasonal workers migrate from farm to farm and crop to crop according to the growing season, so whatever preconceived notions I had about what I should expect for the next few months vanished. There was no job harvesting crops where I'd been working before because the seasons had just changed. This was the signal to move on to the next job and employer.

When I went to meet with the foramen at surrounding farms, the majority of the posts had already been filled. They were pleased by my ability to repair machinery and drive anything on wheels, but these skilled, supervisory jobs were normally achieved only after several periods of climbing the corporate ladder. I knew that no matter where I landed or what season or crop I was in, I'd have to get used to beginning over every time I moved. And with each relocation, I'd have to get to know a new boss, who had to report to a new owner, as well as find my position in a new group of coworkers. The only thing that remained consistent, whether the crop was cotton, tomatoes, maize, cauliflower, broccoli, grapes, or melons, all of which I assisted in cultivating during the next eighteen months, was that one or two of the workers remembered me as Doc.

Fortunately for me, after a few days with Uncle Fausto, I was hired on at one of the massive nearby ranches. For the next few weeks, I lived in my car, effectively homeless, until I had saved enough money to proudly pay $300 for my first home-a small camping trailer I could park at whichever farm employed me, not far from where other migrant workers were housed during busier seasons.

I discovered many nearly unfixable leaks on the first or second night of living in the trailer. This corresponded with my realisation that the winter cold in Mendota was far more uncomfortable than in the Baja. Clearly, I was unprepared for the bone-chilling wetness of those freezing evenings and early mornings, especially as I struggled to adjust to a far more strenuous work schedule than I had previously encountered. But I wasn't willing to acknowledge defeat, so I chose to embrace, even relish, the difficulties and view them as instructional. Who am I to be concerned about the weather and admit to feeling more alone than I have ever felt in my life? There is no way. And to prove it to myself, I chose to appreciate my leaking trailer's flaws-not to mention its ugly, uncomfortable blue-green trim. I remained my father's son. So be it if the weather was chilly and the labour was difficult. My thinking was that I was being tested-physically and mentally-and that if I could successfully complete this pass, nothing could stop me. I could live with that if something happened to shake my confidence. I would win if I could fight back by dismissing the situation as insignificant. That's how I choose to see my leaking trailer: as a palace, not as the trappings of poor me!

Then I discovered that the seasonal obligation of shifting irrigation lines was one of the most menial and difficult chores for any agricultural worker. Wouldn't you agree? That was my winter job-the first challenge thrown at me, just in time to bring me back to earth. To others, this trial by fire may have been nothing more than a decision to accept a position that no one else wanted. But it would have been defeatist of me. Instead, I needed to figure out how to handle it and flourish at it. My source of inspiration? Bruce Springsteen, defender of the working class, whose "Born in the USA" had already become an anthem for me, despite the fact that I wasn't born in the country. To demonstrate my tough independence, I purchased an all-terrain vehicle, a Honda 175 motorcycle (red, my new favourite colour), and a rarely seen three-wheeler-both of which I could drive in the fields and on the road.

Moving irrigation lines was far more difficult than I had imagined. The objective was to move twenty-yard-long parts of the lines from one row of cotton seedlings to the next, taking them up at one end and then shifting them bit by bit at the other. The terrain was a horrible mixture of mud and quicksand. Anyone wearing boots or shoes would slide into knee-deep mud and get trapped. I could walk twice as fast barefoot, but I still fell to my knees in the muck, and my feet were immediately torn to shreds, becoming freezing and bloody. And it was pretty much my entire day, every day, in the cold. Brutal!

The physical toll included exhaustion, discomfort, and a lot of pain, but the real challenge was confronting my fear of discomfort, my dread that the hours would elapse too slowly, my resistance to the sheer monotony of repetition and menial labour, my insecurity that others would look down on me because I worked in the dirt, and my own maddening impatience for the work to be done.

I survived at first by daydreaming about my unfolding master plan to make a lot of money quickly and return to my country triumphant-no longer the child of a poor family or a teacher who couldn't afford to do the job for which he was trained, but a man of stature, wealth, and options. However, after a few paychecks, this fantasy started to wear thin. With my hourly income of $3.75-50 more than the minimum wage at the time-I realised I'd need much more than a year or two to collect the kind of funds I'd hoped to accumulate in that time.

So I told myself that I would not be working on these California farms for the rest of my life; my employment on these farms was merely the first step toward saving enough money to return home and pursue a university education. Other steps would be taken. But, just as crucial as seeing the large picture, I had to learn how to live in the present moment and embody the little picture-how to focus more intensely on whatever work was at hand. I had no idea that learning to wield this sword of intense, pure attention would come in handy later in life, from adjusting irrigation lines to picking tomatoes to battling brain cancer.

I discovered that with focus came patience-a commodity I'd never had in plenty. And, oddly, it was my patience that allowed me to advance quickly at each subsequent position. Patience, which is required for both crop cultivation and Nobel Prize-winning research, fostered delight and a love of life. Of course, without joy, we are left with drudgery and even hopelessness. Passion inspired me to do my best, no matter how tiny or insignificant the task. Some may think I'm insane for having a penchant for field work. But I grew to appreciate the effort as a gem I had discovered in the San Joaquin Valley, one that would make me rich for life and make me feel like the alpha guy I desired to be. This was my time in the sun, my chance to shine, and I wasn't going to let the cruel, frigid winter, irrigation lines, or leaky trailers stop me.

And I did rise. By the end of the season, I had progressed from shifting irrigation lines to driving one of the biggest, baddest, most intricate pieces of farm equipment of the time. It looked like a space-age dragon and could nearly fly, able to plough earth in huge swaths-provided, of course, that the driver could handle it with extreme precision. I liked driving that dragon, sitting up in the cab with my coffee and breakfast, seeing the steam rise from the hot thermos and my breath escape into the frigid air as I battled a pack of cunning coyotes desperate to climb into the cab and steal my food. When the winter season ended in late March, I returned to the team working for Uncle Fausto. I was inspired to learn some of the history of this Greek family while visiting the ten-thousand-acre family-owned ranch that had been founded during the Great Depression. I discovered that the owner's grandfather had come to Ellis Island and migrated west, starting as a seasonal farm labourer and working his way up until he had enough money to start his own small farm here in the heart of central California. It was amazing to envision the stages of growth of that first harvest and the crops blossoming over the years so that future generations of his family may benefit from his ambition. Where else could such a success story be recounted than in America? What was to stop me from one day owning my own ranch? Nothing!

Nothing, except that if I rose to the top of the class at one job, the slate was wiped clean when I went on to the next, and I had to start over. Fortunately, I rose quickly, sometimes on a daily basis, sometimes within a week, until I was in charge of a team. This development reminded me that, while patience was a virtue, I preferred forward motion-like the rapid stars I admired in the night sky. But, whether moving slowly or quickly, I had numerous doubts. One such occurrence caught me off guard during a lunch break when I decided to talk in Spanish with the child behind the counter at the small market in the middle of nowhere. By this point, I had purchased my first Spanish-English dictionary (which I kept in my hip pocket at all times) and had even begun a journal in which I was attempting to record my thoughts in my very bad English. Most of the time, I ordered my lunch in English and had no response from the adolescent who worked there, who was clearly Mexican-American- probably first generation.

On this particular day, being my natural, sociable nature, I remarked something in Spanish about the lovely spring weather and then concluded with, "Have a pleasant afternoon, brother." The child glared back at me in disgust, saying nothing. No, his expression was mocking. Even mockery. I felt as upset as I did when I was six years old and the big kids played marbles with me and stole money from the gas station cash register. When I evaluated the market encounter, I recognized that the teenager's guilt about our common ethnicity had less to do with me and more to do with his humiliation about his parents, who could have been migrant labourers. I've got it. But his reaction instilled in me, for the first time, a sense of nervousness about my accent and being Mexican. Even though it was unwelcome, the small thing quickly took root.

Shortly after, I was out in the field one day, assisting one of the guys on my team, when the son of one of the owners went by and looked my way, but showed no sign of having noticed the existence of another human being. That was how he saw all of the labourers. Were we unnoticed? Did he not notice that we were there, doing everything we could to bring in his family's harvest, raise its earnings, and enrich him as well? We were not individuals with names or identities in his eyes; we were nonentities, even faceless.

I wanted to give him the benefit of the doubt, but another incident made it difficult. Our paths crossed again when I was given the opportunity for extra labour in the evenings and on weekends-cleaning the young man's family's ranch house. Later, I would see other magnificent mansions, but when I arrived at the property and stood outside, the huge home appeared to be from Lifestyles of the Rich and Famous. I rang the doorbell, nervous and excited. I tried knocking when no one came to open the door. Nothing. Finally, I rang again, and the same irritated adolescent threw open the door. He pointed to the cleaning materials, motioned to the main portion of the home, and left me to fend for myself. I came to the conclusion that migrant labourers were seen as not just faceless but also mute.

Later, I could reflect on these meetings and see the early lessons they had taught me about the importance of compassion and caring for the many patients who are all too frequently treated as faceless and voiceless in institutional and even familial settings. The treatment of migrant workers also served as a reminder to recognize the contributions of everyone in the hospital, clinic, or lab, from orderlies and janitors to nurses and technicians, and all the way up to doctors and administrators. Every person has a name, a face, and a voice. And these marginalisation experiences would prevent me from seeing others solely through the lens of their work or diagnosis—as anything less than a fully alive person and valuable human being.

One unusually hot summer afternoon, I was hurried to the cornfield with urgent screams of, "Get Doc, tell him to hurry, his uncle Mario has collapsed!" Everyone knew I wasn't a doctor now. But, because

Uncle Mario was my father's brother and had come up from Ensenada to work during the busy season, I was the natural choice.

It wasn't difficult for me to conclude that dehydration had played a role in my uncle's collapse. He was going to be OK with water and salt tablets. Nonetheless, I believed he should be examined by a licensed physician. When I spoke with Asunción-"Chon," as we called him on the job site-he stared at me like I was crazy. What about medical care for migrant workers?

This was not just about my uncle. He hadn't suffered a heart attack or a stroke, for sure. But, then, what if he hadn't? We lacked access and advocates. We're naked out here, I recall thinking, absolutely vulnerable, less than nothing. Uncle Mario, it seemed, felt the same way. He collected his belongings and returned to Ensenada not long after his breakdown.

In and of itself, these occurrences had little effect on my drive to accomplish well for myself. I was still convinced that I had arrived in the ultimate land of possibility. But I was starting to realise that without an education, hard labour would not be enough to get ahead. This lesson was reinforced anytime I met Cousin Fausto, who was doing well at Fresno State. He attributed his success to the lovely young lady he had met and was about to marry. He had connected to God and religion via her influence in a way that would lead him from then on. Fausto, I may add, always seemed spiritually connected. He was a tenacious, endlessly generous soul who was always looking out for others.

"You know," Fausto suggested six months into my adventure as a migrant worker, "you should take some classes at Fresno State." It would be beneficial to your social life!"

"I'd love that," I said. "But I don't know where I'd find the time." In addition, my application for a worker's authorization, which was required to attend college, had not yet been accepted.

The good news was that, in the aftermath of President Ronald Reagan's 1986 amnesty law, the state of California was revising its stance toward migrant farm labourers. You qualified for a worker's authorization if you could demonstrate that you had worked in the United States for a specific number of days in the preceding year. You could then apply for a temporary green card, followed by a permanent green card. So, once I acquired a work permit, my intention was to enrol in night classes to enhance my English. Meanwhile, I'd have to rely on my pocket dictionary. Because of the shifting regulations governing migrant labour, more of my family members were able to join me in the San Joaquin Valley by July. Rosa and Ramón Ramirez, my sister, were among the first to arrive. They were expecting their first child and hoped Ramón could find a job at the ranch where I was working. Fortunately, he was recruited immediately, and they became my neighbours, parking their spacious (or so I believed at the time), well-insulated trailer near mine.

Even though Ramón was a friend of mine, I was disappointed when I learned that he and my sister were getting married. She was sixteen years old, making her even younger than our parents when they married. But as I got to know Ramón better, I realised she couldn't have picked a finer husband-truly her soul mate. Even before the fatal day in the not-too-distant future when Ramón would assist in saving my life, I had other reasons to admire his strength of heart and commitment.

Soon after the two of them arrived at the ranch, the following wave of family members came, including my parents and my younger siblings, Jorge, thirteen, and Jaqueline, nine. Gabriel had planned to stay in Mexico until he finished his technical college program. I appreciated his decision and knew how difficult it was for him to stay behind on his own, especially since he had moved into our grandparents' house, which had now been converted into a funeral home, to save money on rent. Discuss ghost stories!

I could tell Mamá wasn't ready for the changes that had transpired in me during our time apart from the minute I rushed across the muddy field on my three-wheeler to greet them. But she didn't say anything except that she was glad to see me.

Years later, Mamá acknowledged feeling distressed that day. "To see your face dirty from the mud and working in the fields," she added, "it made me sad." You'd trained to be a teacher. You had graduated three years before everyone else. "You had changed, and it wasn't how I expected to see you," she told Uncle Fausto later that night.

"What exactly do you mean?""My uncle inquired.

"He had dirt on his face, was sunburned, and was wearing mud-caked jeans." But I know it's only for a little time."

"Flavia, your son has a future here," my uncle stated. That's how he'll always appear."

My mother was so terrified by his statements that she decided not to inform me. But his declaration that I would not resume my course toward a career outside of field labour had so disappointed her that she later said, "All my hopes began to go down."

When Papá saw me returning at the ranch, he must have felt conflicted emotions as well. He may be proud that I was climbing the ranks, but he had to realise that I was far from the world of books and learning that he desired for me. Then again, I wasn't really interested in what he wanted. Probably I was still furious that he hadn't done more to improve our family's situation after the economic challenges had brought us down so far. I suppose that my fury drove me at times to prove that it was possible to get back up after being knocked down, that sometimes a man needs to do what a man has to do. But, no matter what, I adored my father and lamented the fact that he seemed to have lost his will to pursue his destiny.

Mamá and Papá soon departed the ranch, deciding to travel farther north to pursue work in the more industrial area of Stockton, on the northern edge of the San Joaquin Valley. They expected Jorge and Jaqueline to do better in the schools there. Rosa and her family soon chose to travel to Stockton as well. When they tried to persuade me to join them, I resisted, claiming that I had some big plans in Mendota, including my own trucking company!

I began to fantasise about my new business, starting small and gradually expanding my fleet, eventually hiring all of my family members, present and future. I'd name the company Q Trucking and emblazon the name on all my trucks with a brilliant yellow comet on a black high-gloss background!

I went to work with my cousin Hector, who claimed to be a mechanic, after making a down payment to Uncle Fausto on an old truck. I was confident that my product-hauling abilities would outperform those of the competition after investing the little money I had saved. As I worked with Hector to repair the vehicle and its engine, I realised how much I appreciated not only the feel of grease on my hands, but also using both my brain and my hands at the same time. Even though I wasn't on the path to school, I wasn't completely lost. I was investigating different routes in pursuit of fulfilment, pleasure, challenges, and adventure, as Tata Juan had pushed me to do.

Except for the unusual noises the truck was making, everything else my business venture went swimmingly.

"It's nothing, don't worry!" Hector reassured me."

So I wasn't concerned until I was travelling down Highway 99 with a truckload of broccoli and noticed a tire roll in front of me. Who in their right mind would blow a tire on this crowded highway? The response came soon. I skidded into a ditch with a clang and a bang, vegetables flying all over the road.

"What kind of mechanic are you?"" When I saw Hector, I questioned him.

He shrugged apologetically, "Not a bad one?""

So much for the trucking industry. With my finances depleted, I returned to the Greek family's ranch for the fall and winter seasons, weeding and collecting cotton from the ground up. But before the winter was out, I'd gone to the top again, ploughing the fields and racing the coyotes in the enormous dragon Caterpillar, the massive John Deere tractors, the intimidating cotton picker, and the space-age tomato picker suitable for an astronaut.

By the spring season, my brown corduroy wallet was once again bulging with uncashed checks, my work authorization papers were in order, and I had been promoted yet again-this time to the third in charge. Not too shabby. And it was in this setting that I had a life-changing chat with my cousin Oscar one afternoon.

Oscar, a gorgeous young guy with a strong, square jaw, would go on to further his schooling and become a teacher. But, at the time, he was preoccupied with climbing the ranch's success ladder and boosting his income by hauling melons with his own vehicle.

Oscar didn't seem to have his older brother's or my sense of adventure or fun. Oscar was as clever, tenacious, and diligent as the rest of the Hinojosa family, but he was sceptical of anything that seemed unduly ambitious. In any case, when I announced my recent plan to enrol in night school to enhance my English, he became immediately gloomy. He may not have comprehended the extent of my uneasiness over my thick accent and inadequate language skills, but he must have known that without more education, I would be stuck struggling at a subsistence level. Nonetheless, he seemed personally upset by my plans.

Nothing could diminish the knowledge I had gained in the fields. It had been a blessing, and I had learnt from the best-the everyday heroes who till the soil and reap the crop. As a year-round employee, I had experienced the delight of harvesting a tomato from a vine I had grown. But, at the age of twenty, I couldn't accept that I'd reached the height of what a field labourer could achieve. With a degree, I envisaged myself in a management position at one of the major food corporations-why not? Then, after earning some real money, I'd return to Mexico with the freedom to have, be, and do anything I wanted. And the first step in realising this lovely ambition was to improve my English.

Oscar initially remained silent. But then he began to laugh, as if laughing were the only acceptable reaction to my apparent insanity. "Don't delude yourself!" Finally, he said. "Are you going to school to learn English?" C'mon."

I didn't respond at first, and I let his remark pass me by. Oscar had been through his own difficulties, dealing with his parents' divorce at a young age, but it occurred to me in this case that he didn't really understand what it was like to live in poverty or go without access to the opportunities and education that living in the United States provided-including the freedom to believe in and pursue the American dream. So I ignored his laughs and said nothing.

Oscar then turned solemn. "Look," he pointed out, "you don't need a dictionary or night classes." Why squander your time? You've completed in a year and a half what Chon took eleven years to accomplish. You're already at the top of the food chain!"

I felt a tingle of fear start in my stomach and go through me while still not saying anything.

"This is where you're supposed to be, Freddy," Oscar continued.

You'll be the foreman before you know it!"

I couldn't catch my breath because my heart was pounding like a bass drum in my ears. I've got it. Of course, I did. He wanted me to take my head out of the clouds, to keep me from overthinking things and setting myself up for disappointment. But in doing so, he was snuffing out the hopes of that little child who had stood on his roof with a slingshot, attempting to hit a star.

"Look at where you are," he added again, admiringly, "you belong here." You'll always be working in the fields. You're not going anywhere. You'll be working in the fields for the rest of your life."

When I heard that horrible comment, I felt as if Oscar had sliced me open and taken my heart in his hands, squeezing it with all his power. Even now, I can recall my bodily reaction at the time: my heart was crushed by the weight, power, and conviction of his dreadful prognosis.

Perhaps he was correct. I was never going to leave the fields as long as I stayed there, transfixed, shocked, and hurt—to think otherwise was to delude myself.

There was only one thing to do but stand there like a statue. I told Chon I was going on a break, then jumped on my three-wheeler and flew over the muddy tomato field for the last time, speeding down the dirt road to the next pay phone. Deep down, I knew there were only two options when faced with difficulties: either change them or adjust yourself to meet them. In the end, I had made the correct decision. But, by the time I picked up the phone, the drama of the moment had dissipated, and I understood that the individuals who had believed in me would be disappointed.

I called my folks, who were staying with cousins in Stockton, with my tail between my legs. They agreed without hesitation to come pick me up. Within two days, I'd made plans to leave my trailer behind and store my three-wheeler until I could return. I had forty-eight hours to second-guess my decision, especially because I had no idea what the future contained. I was leaving behind the security of a respectable career as a migrant agricultural labourer in favour of the unknown. The image of this new future was hazy, like if I'd opened a door into a dimly lit room and couldn't find the light switch. I could feel my prior arrogance eroding as I waited for my parents and younger siblings to turn the corner to pick me up.

I began to smile the moment I spotted my father behind the wheel of his newest automotive disaster, a phlegmatic Gremlin he had recently purchased, primarily because he loved the colour, an awful mustard yellow. The ugly mustard yellow Gremlin was the most gorgeous sight in the world at the time.

We loaded a handful of my items into the hatchback and embarked on an unbelievable journey. As we drove out of Mendota and I looked back at the rusting train tracks that had brought me all the way from the outskirts of Palaco, Mexico, and were now carrying us north, I marvelled at the audacious, naive nineteen-year-old who had arrived here a lifetime ago. I had to start afresh. I didn't hear a single critique or question about what had transpired or about crushed expectations and dreams. In fact, the atmosphere in the car was jubilant! Soon after, someone cracked a joke, and a series of funny stories and anecdotes ensued. We were laughing so hard that we were wiping our eyes and holding our sides in no time.

The singing then began. And we had to deal with the Gremlin's eccentricities. To avoid overheating, Papá had to pull over every thirty minutes or so and pour water into the radiator, as well as add oil each time.

We were having so much fun travelling at no more than fifty miles per hour that we didn't care if it took us five hours to complete what should have been a two-hour excursion. I remembered those earlier excursions to the Sea of Cortez and how they would stay with me long after I'd returned home as we drove into the rough streets of Stockton, searching the signs for our new address. Similarly, this lovely excursion would linger in my heart for a long time, allowing me to securely cross the border from everything that had come before to whatever was to come next.

My participation in night programs at San Joaquin Delta College marked the beginning of a period of tremendous growth and learning for me. The next order of business was to find work. Although my new work could have been considered as a step down the food chain, when I was hired to shovel sulphur at the port, I figured it was simply another test, not a permanent punishment.

Moving irrigation lines had been a piece of cake in comparison to my port duties! The smell of sulphur, which began to live inside my nostrils and coat my clothes, skin, and hair, is not an easily forgotten sense memory. The odour is frequently compared to that of rotten eggs, raw sewage, or a bad case of flatulence. It's no coincidence that descriptions of hell include fire and brimstone, often known as sulphur.

However, thanks to a few key purchases, getting to and from this work in hell was pure bliss. After saving up about $7,000, I was able to purchase two items I'd previously only dreamed of: first, a pair of Ray-Ban sunglasses, and second, a brand-new red Nissan minitruck, my first car that had never been owned by anyone else.

Over the next few weeks, I became a regular at Pep Boys, investing my sulphur-shovelling wages in souping up my no-frills truck until it became my vision of the ultimate American vehicle. I was the dude with several speakers for my car sound and a kit system that allowed me to lower the automobile in time with the music! To demonstrate my cosmopolitan side, I hung fuzzy dice in the front window and a plush animal-a striped, orange, smiling Garfiel-in the back window of the cab.

I straddled two spots whenever I parked the vehicle at work or at the community college to prevent getting dented or dinged. I received a lot of glances with my hair long and a couple of Native American earrings dangling from one ear, blasting tracks ranging from Guns N' Roses to James Brown, much like I did when I sprinted around campus in heavy work boots and splotchy overalls, holding a stack of books in my arms like a baby.

I was mostly unaware of the impression I was creating, but when a friend caught me getting out of the truck, he said, "Vato, none of this computes." But what about Garfield? So, what's your story?"

For nearly two years, my tale had been that once I made it big, I would return to Mexico. But, in reality, I could feel a fresh pull compelling me to contemplate establishing roots here. The mere concept shocked me into accepting the harsh reality that none of my previous plans had worked out. All this time, I had put off returning home because of self-imposed deadlines and the fear that others would regard me as a failure if I didn't have any money or significant accomplishments to show for my time in the United States. The only way to move over failure and fear, I realised, was to return to Mexico and see how I felt. So why not? I suddenly decided to do it in the midst of a Friday afternoon at the port, with only four hours till the shift was done! After work, I'd shower, change, and then get in my ride and drive through the night and into the morning with my legal documents in place, storming into Mexicali with my music blasting and my minitruck rocking out to the beat! Then I'd drive down to Palaco, past the old gas station, and down to Gabriel's grandparents' house to surprise him. Why hadn't I considered this before? Trip via car!

Fatigue came in early in the drive, but I adjusted as the hours and miles passed. The night was memorable for its darkness, with clouds covering the stars and rain looming. The further I travelled from my home in California, the more anxious I became about our shaky hold on any type of security. The path ahead appeared to be as hazy as it had been when I initially crossed the border. Why was life still so difficult?

But, just as the first rays of sunlight appeared, I felt a weird easing of this load. The change was minor, but I welcomed it just as much as the sight of rolling fields of farmland curving down through the valley as I turned east, with the sunrise casting bands of golden light and illuminating areas here and there.

As the sun rose, I felt rejuvenated and comfortable, certain in my belief that anything was possible. And just when my mind was running wild with huge plans for the future, I noticed a VW van in my rearview mirror. I nodded confidently to myself, expecting to see hippies within, holdovers from the society that had reigned in previous years, being familiar with American culture by now-or so I thought. Instead, as the VW van passed me, I noticed two persons, a man and a woman, peering out the back window. But then I took a closer look and discovered those pale circles in the window weren't faces. They were completely naked butts! What? Why would someone perpetuate such a thing on God's green earth?

I didn't discover about the common American prank known as "mooning" until much later, while watching an Eddie Murphy comedy; clearly, I had a lot more to learn about American culture. In the end, I was still a Baja country lad.

But after thirty-six hours back in my hometown, I felt less connected than ever to the place where I grew up. The first indication that I would not be greeted home as a homecoming hero came when I stopped for lunch in Mexicali and returned to my pickup to find that the side glass had been broken and my Garfield had been stolen!

It was fantastic to see Gabriel again and discover that he would soon be joining the rest of the family in Stockton. I was also amused by how easy it was to revert to old patterns of interaction with family and friends. Everyone seemed to be the same as they had always been, except for me. When I ran into my ex-girlfriend, I felt relieved that she had gone on and was in a new, happy relationship; she had moved on and was in a new, happy relationship. Years later, she would tell me that she understood my departure, that she thought I was going somewhere extraordinary, "somewhere none of us had dreamed."

On the trip back to Northern California, I felt that my visit home had provided me with closure. I needed to reconnect with my roots in the land where I grew up. My home turf, on the other hand, appeared narrow and provincial, a place where I could no longer flourish. Nothing was definitively resolved. But one thing became clearer than ever: I needed to push past the boundaries of my education in order to broaden my knowledge.

So, following my return to Stockton, my first item of business was to get out the community college catalogue and circle three classes that seemed interesting. Because none of them were available in the evening, I had to figure out how to alter my schedule with another employment to accommodate them.

Meanwhile, I went back to shovelling sulphur and scraping fish lard-the fatty layer of guts that forms at the bottom of ship tankers, creating a sludge with a sticky smell that is arguably worse than the sulphur's rotten-egg smell, something inconceivable. I joked that I must have been insane to leave the fields-but I wasn't!

The most difficult challenge was suffering the slights of two coworkers who seemed to go out of their way to make me feel inferior to them. One in particular made no attempt to hide his disdain. Despite the fact that he was Chicano, most likely second- or third-generation Mexican-American, he clearly despised my background and ability to advance in the sulphur-shovelling profession. In any event, he didn't hold back when it came to making insulting remarks about my origins south of the border, designating me a "wetback" and embellishing the phrase with additional stereotypical adjectives like "stupid," "lazy," or "dirty."

While his insults increased my uneasiness, I was curious as to why he detested me so much, especially because he was also of Mexican origin. Perhaps he was bothered by my long hair and earrings. Perhaps he despised my sense of humour and my attempts to elicit a chuckle from him and his sneering sidekick by joking that my slender physique had rippling muscles like Rambo's. Given the area's history of racial violence, I wondered if they had developed a dislike for the old country at home or in their neighbourhoods.

When my family moved to Stockton, one of the first things we learned was that it had recently been named the most violent city in America, according to a television news story. Young, disenfranchised Hispanic gang members, as well as African-American gangs and other cliques made up of newer arrivals from Southeast Asia, were engaged in full-fledged combat. Drugs, firearms, and poverty had all contributed to a soaring crime rate, which we had unintentionally walked into while looking for permanent jobs in and around the Port of Stockton.

I'm not sure why none of us youngsters were attracted to gangs or narcotics. One explanation was most likely the strong foundation my parents instilled in each of us, which kept us from being drawn into such terrible activities. At the same time, only Gabriel and I pursued higher education. Our younger siblings, who grew up in Stockton, didn't value further education as much, possibly because of the tumultuous atmosphere that pervaded school and the streets.

We were all vulnerable to the threat of street violence. This became evident to me one Thursday morning as I was driving off to work. In my haste to get a bag of cashews and a soft drink (the lunch of champions back then), I carelessly zipped in front of a massive white vehicle with dark-tinted windows, unwittingly cutting it off. I parked and was ready to walk inside the market when I noticed the white truck driving up next to me and the driver's window sliding down to reveal a large barrel of a rifle placed firmly between my eyes.

"You're going to die!"" yelled the one with the rifle. The frightening clack of the trigger being cocked followed.

My heart rate slowed. My breathing came to a halt. And it appears that the region of the brain that governs bowel processes did as well! I didn't have time to feel embarrassed since I was helpless. But, as I prepared to bid farewell to life, my assailant delivered a severe warning: "Don't EVER cut me off again!""

The pistol was gone, the tinted window was rolled up, and the white vehicle sped out of the parking lot. After catching my breath, I praised God for once again sparing my life and promised to become far more streetwise than my previous experiences had prepared me to be.

After all, I'd grown up in a rural setting, not even a hamlet, in a third-world country, and had spent the majority of my time in America working in the fields. Many adaptations were required for city living. My parents, younger siblings, and I were first crammed into a single room with twin beds in an apartment complex where we shared a bathroom with ten other families. We rented a little house that fit the entire family, as well as Rosa, Ramón, and their lovely infant daughter, Daisy, my first niece, after Gabriel successfully completed college and went north to join us.

My father struggled to adjust to city life. He had little issue finding short-term manual labour jobs, but they weren't stepping stones to something better. Papá, on the other hand, found his outlet in fixing up and painting our leased house, quickly transforming it into a wonderful, colourful home in the centre of an otherwise terrible neighbourhood. My mother remained the family's rock, a genuinely hopeful realist. If my life had been difficult in the past, it was nothing compared to Mamá's. Despite our difficulties, she was able to find constant work, generally in some type of quality control at nearby industries. Mamá could have become an executive at any of those companies with her education. Even lacking the means for such advancements, her advice was frequently sought by coworkers and family alike.

My mother was definitely a sounding board for me, especially when I had to deal with the prejudice of my two coworkers. Her suggestions for dealing with intolerance were so brilliant that I later interviewed her for a college anthropology thesis. When discussing cultural bias, she mentioned some people's urge to consider others as inferior to them.

"I do not think there is such a thing as an inferior or superior race," she was quoted as saying. "However, I am perfectly aware that there is racial discrimination and injustice, not only in the United States, but also throughout the world." Mamá agreed that discrimination would always be a part of life due to ingrained beliefs that allowed some civilizations to consider other cultures as inferior. However, she saw a way ahead for individuals who had been treated as second-class citizens. "I believe that becoming educated is the only way to gain respect." The only way to achieve harmony in the system is to become system leaders rather than victims of injustice."

Just when I was about to give up on fish-lard scraping and sulphur shovelling, my buddy Gustavo-Gus for short-who was married to my mother's cousin told me about an opportunity. A team of welders from California Railcar Repair, a company that renovated tankers that transported commodities discharged from shipyards to various industrial destinations, happened to be less than a hundred feet away from where we shovelled sulphur. Gus was a foreman for the corporation at a different location. This information provided an opportunity for my brother-in-law, Ramón, who had been trained as a welder in Mexico.

Despite his tiny, wiry physique of 112 pounds, Ramón immediately proved to be a great asset with his welding talents and extraordinary power. Gus quickly followed suit and put in a good word for me. Gustavo, who is charming, tall, and brawny, could have been an action-movie star if he had chosen that road. Instead, he had become a great welder like his stepfather, Don Mateo, as we affectionately called him. Gus and Ramón gained permission to train me as a welder after convincing his supervisors to hire me as a cleaner in the shed. I was therefore able to suggest my father take over as janitor.

I received a rude awakening regarding the perils of the profession and the importance of even the tiniest aspects before I had mastered my training. On this particular occasion, I failed to properly apply the eye shield and burned my corneas, causing agonising pain for which the only remedy was to lie in the dark with moist cloths over my eyes. Enough was enough. When I returned to working with the welding iron, I had to learn to keep a respectful distance from the burning, melting lava that I was forging-melding pieces together and pulling others apart, building out the molten substance, playing with it, watching the intense red of the flame's core turn metal into liquid-all while keeping a respectful distance from danger. Such lessons in the careful use of equipment and protective measures would subsequently be applied in surgical settings, though I was unaware of this fate. Nonetheless, I began to feel that a bright future was just around the corner, ready to be discovered.

Then, on April 14, 1989, my promising future came crashing down as I fell to the bottom of the railway tank and failed to crawl out-as I lay unconscious, without oxygen, face down, dying.

Of course, I remember that moment not from direct experience, but from narratives given to me years later by people who were there- accounts that were as difficult for them to deliver as they were for me to hear.

My father's worst nightmares came true the moment he saw Pablo's face and realised my coworker had let go of my hand. When Papá heard the thud resonating in the tank, his shouts were temporarily muted as he was joined by Ramón on one side and Gus, who was bringing ropes and a collapsible ladder, on the other. They had arrived in time to restrain Papá as they peered down to discover that I had fallen with my knees slightly bent under me, my body in a foetal position. I can only imagine my father's desperation, knowing he was so close to being able to save me. According to all reports, including his own, he went insane, and with the sound of Don Mateo praying loudly at the side of the tracks, my father lurched forward, seeking to join the tank, thrashing and assaulting the others who tried to calm him down. The more they tried to reason with him, stressing that if he went in, he would die, the more Papá resisted their attempts to restrain him. Gus warned my father that he was too broad-shouldered to squeeze through the gap, let alone too old to risk the rescue. Thinking back to how Papá must have felt when he heard this, I can't imagine how I would respond if someone told me that I couldn't try to save my children's lives.

Gus wanted to come in as well, but he was far too large to fit through the hole.

Ramón was the one who pushed himself to the front, declaring, "I'm going in." "I'm going in!" he cried, seeing the others' hesitancy. Freddy is dead down there!"

Gus, knowing he could lose both of us, decided that Ramón, who was strong, wiry, and swift, was the only one who had a chance. Gus tied a rope for Ramón and told the team at the top to prepare to throw down the thin metal ladder. Ramón slid down the rope as quickly as he could. Halfway down, the fumes began to overpower him, like being kicked in the stomach, as he subsequently described the sensation. When he landed next to me, he blacked out for a time but managed to revive himself long enough to lift me onto my back, face up. My mouth was foaming, my tongue was protruding, and my skin was going purple. Ramón began to lose consciousness once more, and he realized he needed to go soon if he was to survive. Gus reached down with one hand, grabbed Ramón by the scruff of his neck, and hauled him out like a little animal as he ascended the thin metal ladder that had been dropped in for him. Ramón had passed out by this point. However, as soon as Gus placed him on the upper deck, Ramón began to pound the tanker with his fist, slapping himself awake and alert-exerting enough energy to push the others aside and insisting on going back in.

Ramón descended faster this time, with a rope tied across his chest and another rope to help pull me up. He knew that about ten minutes had passed since I had originally entered the tank, and that due to the lack of oxygen at the bottom, I should have died by now. Ramón was also aware that he only had a few seconds to act before collapsing as well. In those few seconds, he skillfully wrapped the rope around my middle, balancing the weight of my lower limbs with the weight of my torso and head when I was brought up. I'm not sure how he calculated the physics of this manoeuvre-other than that he must have tapped into his superhuman talents, exhibiting not only tremendous strength, agility, and daring, but also a level of intellect. Ramón amazingly made it over the last loop of the rope without passing out. However, once he began ascending for the second time, all of his faculties faded and he was pulled out unconscious once more.

Gus took over and began the laborious task of reeling me up, inch by inch, without making any sudden or hurried movements that would cause an imbalance and send me plummeting again. One slip, one blunder would have been fatal. Gus might have been a brain surgeon, a conductor of a world-class orchestra, or a general organizing his soldiers with this orchestration of difficult moves to save my life. He was all of that and more, performing to the best of his ability—on my behalf.

Papá, Ramón, Pablo, and others were right there to help, with Don Mateo still praying and another team preparing the forklift that would set me down on the ground so I could be loaded into the back of Gus's Ford Bronco and driven to a nearby industrial clinic, where a waiting ambulance would rush me to the nearest hospital. Because our site was so isolated, the roads weren't even marked on area maps, thus explaining where we were to an ambulance driver would have been pointless. As a result, this idea was also a triumph of quick, brilliant thought.

Ramón and Papá, according to the account, never left my side and began to notice signs of life in me during the ambulance ride—a couple of times when I tried to talk but was too bewildered to make any sense. Though I remember trying to wake up, as one does when trying to wake up from a nightmare, I only remember a few blurry images of being transferred into the ambulance and strapped down. My first conscious memory is of opening my eyes, looking around, and finding myself in the hospital on a yellow transport table, flanked by my father and Ramón and a young olive-skinned, large-nosed man dressed in white. I assumed I'd died and gone to heaven, and this man was an angel. But I soon discovered he was a doctor, and I found myself in a hospital for the first time in my life. I had returned to true terra firma-the land of the living-safe and alive.

I was more nauseous than I had ever been in my life, with a terrible taste in my mouth and an awful smell that I couldn't get rid of. My stomach was also in bad shape, churning with an empty, sick feeling. In addition, I was becoming agitated, fighting the restraints of the yellow stretcher and attempting to stand up.

"Relax," the doctor told me, "what's your name?"

"Relax? I can't breathe!" While I fought the impulse to puke, I also began to relax myself and allowed the young emergency department physician to monitor my heart rate and set up an oxygen tent.

A series of medical tests followed. To the shock of everyone involved, the results showed no trace of oxygen deprivation or physical trauma. A few hours passed before I could form coherent sentences, but my father knew I was going to be fine when I noticed some very attractive female nurses and whispered to him, "Does my hair look okay?" Papá laughed in relief.

Nothing had been lost. On the contrary, in the days and weeks that followed, I came to the conclusion that I was more myself than I had ever been, if such a thing was possible. My brush with death seemed to have rewired and supercharged my brain, allowing my instincts and senses to operate at a higher level. I felt as if, in the moments when I had battled for my life, the adrenaline needed for survival had risen to a permanently higher level, intensifying my focus and helping me turn negative energy into more positive results. Mysterious, I know, but it's a phenomenon I would observe time and again in patients and others who must fight against their own mortality.

In the meantime, no one could understand why I didn't break any bones when I fell so suddenly after letting go of Pablo's hand. Was I just lucky? Well, that can be debated. But as for the heroism of Ramón, Gus, my father, and everyone else who played their part in saving my life, that was more than luck. And yet, because of the trauma and my fear that talking or even thinking about the event would conjure negativity, more years than I care to recall would pass before I could bring myself to raise the subject and thank them personally.

Papá was the only one to comment on the miracle as such. "You have been given a gift," he told me at the hospital. "Put it to use, Freddy. Life is short. Be good to others."

Perhaps seeing the doctor's example, as he stood by and provided the safety I needed, helped open my eyes to my father's meaning, even if I didn't make the connection. When I arrived home the next day, everyone could see at once that I was all right but needed to be alone. No one asked any questions when I went into our little living room to sit by myself in quiet solitude.

We had just moved into the house and had no furniture yet, so I sat on the hardwood floor-barefoot and without a shirt, just in my jeans-in a state of such intense introspection that I can still see, smell, hear, and feel every tiny detail of that night: the chilly evening air, the smell of the wood varnish on the floor, the noise of dinnertime and random conversations in the neighbourhood, the sound of tires rumbling by on the asphalt, the mix of music from car stereos with the bass turned up high-all booming and drowning out the sound of my weeping.

Twenty-one years old, still with no facial hair (though I was determined to have a goatee once I got a chin whisker or two), I let myself cry it out. This was the first time that I had cried throughout the ordeal, and my tears were part relief, part gratitude, and part delayed trauma from having seen death and come back.

As I sat there, thinking of my father's words about the gift I'd been given, I felt overwhelmed. And in that moment, I decided never to think of those minutes close to death ever again. Whoever I once had been-seeking to prove myself by material means in order to go home a conquering hero-was no more. Instead, I had to go where the path didn't lead and see where it took me, using unprecedented levels of energy to reinvent myself, to move farther and with more passion in order to be who I was and to become who I was meant to be. As if transformed, I no longer cared about the trappings of wealth or dreams of riches that had motivated me before. Something better and more meaningful was out there for me, and I needed to search for it. And with that revelation, I stood up from the floor with a new level of confidence and drive.

Other than the long-postponed conversations that would occur much later on, my journal entry of April 19, 1989, remains the only record of the incident. In this brief mention, I noted that the doctor had told me how lucky I was, that staying at the bottom of the tank as long as I did would have killed most people. If I had been down there two minutes longer, I would have died.

Those two minutes were the gift that every person on the rescue team gave me. My father, I believe, played the pivotal role, amplifying everyone's sense of urgency. He gave me a fighting chance-thanks to his love and devotion and the speed with which he responded to his own premonition. Two minutes. My life!

PART II HARVESTING

In 1999, after Labor Day, in San Francisco, California, I was a young neurosurgery intern at the University of California, San Francisco Hospital, and experienced a terrifying incident. Even though it's only been two months working at one of the busiest level I trauma hospitals in the country, it already feels like it's been a long time.

During one work day, a senior doctor and I were preparing to perform a procedure on a patient with late-stage HIV infection. During this process, an unfortunate accident happened when a large needle containing infected blood pierced my hand. I was taken into the clinic for examination and preparation for a series of tests, as well as the start of treatment with a special medication within a month. Doctors report that only after a year of regular testing will it be possible to know whether the therapy is working, which means another year of living in uncertainty.

I felt hopeless and scared, remembering the time I almost died in a work accident 10 years ago. I began to wonder if I might be lucky to escape death a second time. It felt like I was carrying a ticking time bomb, returning to my job thinking I might have been a dead man walking.

5. Courting Destiny

After the ADIS immunisation days, I pondered on the crises and problems I had attempted to conquer in 1999. He chose to move out and discover a new route ten years ago, in 1989, after surviving a fall into the pool. Working the swing shift at California Railcar Repair allowed me to attend college classes throughout the day. I was now the company's head of a specialised team, making an astounding ten dollars an hour. My mornings were split-second timed drills. I'd get to the library when the doors opened at 6:00 a.m. and study until classes started, at which point I'd rush from one lecture hall to the next, finishing the last class with no time to spare. Then I'd fly outside, hop into the red truck, and screech into the job site in time for the afternoon shift.

On weekends, I began running races for college track-and-field competitions, not because I needed to be busier, but because I needed to burn off the surplus energy that appeared to have increased since the accident. If I had fifteen to twenty minutes to spare in this timetable, I would have my lunch outside in the quad, on a bench or on the grass.

I was so deep in concentration during one lunch break at roughly 11:30 a.m. on a sunny California day that I didn't notice the two lovely young women strolling toward me as I sat on a cement ledge near a fountain and a fish pond filled with vivid orange-red koi. One of the two, a tall, slim eighteen-year-old with long blonde hair and what I would soon notice to be enchanting emerald eyes, had not been as unaware of my presence. In fact, I later found that she had seen me flying across campus several times and had puzzled where I was going in such a hurry, as well as being captivated by my style- the ponytail, the earrings, the paint-splattered trousers, and the Red Wing work boots. How had I missed her-a knockout who oozed intelligence and warmth?

True, I was easily intimidated in social situations at the time, was self-conscious about my accent, and was culturally illiterate. However, this has not prevented me from dating or having romantic connections. Of course, nothing serious. But I was a red-blooded Latin male, so I wasn't completely clueless. On this particular day, however, I was clueless, despite the fact that everything else in my focus was crisp and vivid-the gurgling of the fountain and the splashing of the koi in the pond, the pleasant spring weather, and the dance of students across the quad, many of whom were gathering in small groups to converse, study, laugh, argue, and flirt. I was mostly concerned with my sandwich. But before I could take a mouthful, the two young women (sisters, I subsequently discovered) had invited themselves to sit, one on either side of me.

I sat rigid, bidding farewell to all semblance of assurance. When the tall blonde struck up a discussion, I was too self-conscious about my accent and inadequate English to say anything more than a guttural "Hi" before fleeing. I couldn't wait to get out of there!

Clearly, the two young women mistook me for someone else. So I forgot about the experience. However, a few weeks later, the enchantress approached me as I was standing in the quad with my classmate Mike, discussing a mathematics project. "So, Mike, are you going to introduce me to your friend?" she inquired, slightly tilting her head. "No way," Mike answered. "I'm not going to introduce you two!"

I thought I felt jealousy for a split second before dismissing it; why would he be jealous of me? I later discovered that he had a crush on her and didn't want the competition. None of this made a dent in my thick skull, nor did it occur to me that she was following me in any way.

Even though her route crossed mine frequently, I didn't connect the dots until one day at the school swimming pool, when I was rehabbing a groyne injury I'd sustained on the track. I saw a vision emerge from the pool as I high-stepped through the water, wearing a weighted vest and fiercely pumping my arms, like Venus rising from the half shell.

I just stared at her for a bit, but then the image spoke. "Hi!" I'd seen that smile before, those emerald eyes! But hold on. Was she addressing me? I shifted my gaze to the left. There was no one present. I shifted my gaze to the right. There was no one else there either. She nodded, as if to confirm that she was speaking to her. Once more, "Hello!"

I nodded back, leaped out of the water, made a fast turn, and rushed into the men's locker room, mumbling something that was neither English nor Spanish and was unclear even to me. When my heartbeat finally slowed, I recognized the wonderful young woman who had approached me in the quad and subsequently asked Mike to introduce us. Though I later discovered she was a competitive swimmer and a lifeguard, all I could think of at the time was the remarkable fact that she had just said hello to me. Not just once, but twice. What was she attempting to convey to me?

It would have been a leap to imagine her attention was anything other than platonic. For starters, she was a classic beauty and all-American, possibly of Scandinavian ancestry, but I was Hispanic and foreign born. But it was her cool confidence, her strong sense of self, and her open, inquiring demeanour that convinced me she was out of my league. She was probably far too intelligent for me to compete with her.

Following this encounter, I began to note how frequently she was at the library shortly after I arrived in the early morning. Wow, I'd say this young lady is quite the scholar! When I still didn't grasp the point, she gave up on me and said, "Hey, this man is clueless!" She was certain that I was uninterested.

But, just in case, she approached me again in the quad, this time extending her hand and saying, "Hi, I don't think we've been officially introduced." Anna Peterson is my name."

"How are you, Alfredo?" I asked, grasping her hand. Is it too formal? I quickly added, "But most people call me Freddy."

"I like Alfredo," she was adamant. That was the end of it.

Thank heavens for her tenacity. If I had been left to make the ceremonial introductions, it would have taken considerably longer for me to learn the name of the person who was to be the love of my life and the lady I was meant to marry. But it took another two years for that realisation to sink in.

Meanwhile, we were able to form a friendship without the stress of dating. Anna, I quickly realised, was one of the most loving people I'd ever known, always looking after family members, acquaintances, and even strangers, always concerned about the well-being of others. She had been reared primarily by her mother, a schoolteacher, after her parents split when she was quite young. Anna's father, an oceanographer with a PhD who worked for the California Geological Survey, remarried when she was about eight years old and had two more children, giving her a half sister and a half brother.

Though I could tell she'd been through a lot, Anna wasn't the type to dwell on the negative or wear her problems on her sleeve. Her view was that confronting those problems had made her stronger. This was just speculation on my part because Anna was a profoundly private person, despite the fact that I could tell she was fiercely independent from the start. I was impressed to hear how she had started working at such a young age. In addition to working as a lifeguard, Anna had begun her own swimming lessons at a nearby pool, offering scholarships to youngsters with limited finances or disabilities. She certainly valued family: I could tell how attached she was to her house and how close she was to her mother and elder sisters.

Anna grew up in Manteca, a little rural town south of Sacramento, where she currently lives, and her desire was to become a veterinarian, as she stated casually one day.

"Do you love animals?" I questioned in my halting English, inspired by her ambition.

"Oh, yes," Anna said with a smile. She talked about her pets and the various injured animals she slipped into her house or adopted—birds, cats, snakes, goats, geese, dogs, horses, and pretty much every other species. She decided to pursue a teaching career because it would allow her to find work and start earning a living more quickly. Her goal was to leave the house as quickly as possible.

Despite the fact that Anna and I had grown up in different cultures and nations, I noticed that we shared many values: family, respect and appreciation for others, and fortitude in the face of adversity. Nonetheless, I was too self-conscious to contribute much to the discussion about myself. When we ran into one another, it was simpler to keep a safe distance-a nod, a wave, a smile, and then I was off and running!

I had a twinge of guilt later, when I had started dating someone else and saw Anna with the tall basketball-player boyfriend she was seeing at the time. I had no idea at the time that love not only has the power to vanquish anything, but it also worms its way into our most primal brain activity and, before we realise it, becomes a part of our DNA. Something deep within me was already telling me that we were meant to be together, but it would take some time for the message to reach me.

What did get through were the critical influences of some excellent professors who were less interested with giving me answers and more concerned with challenging me to ask questions-encouraging me to go off the beaten road and investigate stuff for the sole purpose of discovering what was there. The topic matter was not memorable in some circumstances. But there were notable exceptions, such as when I was able to study with Professor Richard Moore, who taught English as well as a life-changing subject called Film as Literature, at least for me.

Professor Moore taught the principles of literary criticism and composition writing in his regular English lectures, providing me the opportunity to begin writing coherently and meaningfully in English, a talent that would be so important throughout my schooling and career. Though he emphasised the necessity of grammar norms and good organisation, he also urged that papers communicate a strong point of view that is adequately supported by clear, substantive reasons. The ability to communicate my own strong point of view on the page was a novel and liberating experience.

Professor Moore, as a mentor, may have understood that movies had already played a significant effect in influencing my viewpoint. He heightened that knowledge by assisting me in appreciating the power of all movies: classic, nonclassic, great, decent, and even awful. Richard Moore appeared more at home in the Ivy League with his glasses, neatly trimmed beard, bow tie, plaid shirt, cardigan sweater, and sports jacket than in the community college auditorium where he taught Film as Literature and screened films like Federico Fellini's La Strada (starring my countryman Anthony Quinn). I avoided his attention in this class of 200 kids because I was in awe of him. But no matter how hard I tried to conceal, slumped in a middle-section seat, he would find me. Perhaps his radar picked up on my ponytail or the metallic train smell of my work clothing.

"So, Mr. Quinones, what do you think of Stanley Kubrick's decision to shoot Dr. Strangelove in black and white?" Professor Moore would begin.

While listening closely, I would try to read his lips and then mentally translate. "I like it very much," I'd whisper hesitantly. "The black and white showed contrast."

He'd scratch his beard and nod, and I doubted he knew what I was saying any more than I did!

But it was because of such confrontations that I was encouraged to enhance my talents in speech and debate class, eventually becoming a team captain. In retrospect, I see that my knowledge of the English language still had a long way to go. In actuality, I wasn't a particularly good debater. But I based my persuasion power on a clear point of view and wasn't hesitant to take a strong stance on an issue while still managing to exploit my flaws. How? My secret weapon was to speak firmly while smiling, knowing that my opponents couldn't understand me very well. Though the judges had my written arguments in front of them and could follow along, my opponents did not and were unable to respond to any of mine. I know that was an unusual approach to win, but it worked.

Perhaps it was because I arrived at community college knowing no one, with no reputation to follow me from previous schooling or from my socioeconomic background, that I had nothing to prove to anyone but myself. The only restriction was the sky. I made the dean's list on a regular basis and joined the honour society and its steering committee since the environment was so conducive to growth and learning. I thought my scholastic days were done when I graduated in the spring of 1991, at the age of twenty-three.

Not so fast, I was told in my final semester. I'd overlooked one important piece of information, as I was surprised to learn when one of my instructors inquired if I'd applied to any universities yet. I didn't comprehend the distinction between an associate degree from a junior college and a degree from a complete four-year program until that point, nor did I understand the distinction between private and public institutions, or between a state college and a highly ranked university. I'd always imagined that community college marked the start and conclusion of secondary education.

"Not really," responded my lecturer. "This is just a start."

How could I have missed this? Was I mistaken in thinking that just because I finished a class in industrial psychology and enjoyed it, the academic aspect was over and the course would catapult me into a lucrative career?

My professor gently stated that such inquiries might be directed to a counsellor at the counselling facility. In fact, he was astonished that I hadn't taken advantage of the advisors' availability sooner.

Not knowing what to do, I made an appointment with an advisor right away and then sought advice from Peter Dye, a classmate and one of my closest friends. Peter was surprised that I hadn't realised there was more education to come. He had previously mentioned the application process, but I had not understood what he was referring to. The lesson was a cautionary one, advising me not to be scared to ask questions if I didn't understand what others were saying in the future.

Peter also admitted that because I was the first member of my family to pursue higher education in the United States, my ignorance of the system made sense to him. But, he said, if I wanted to go into industrial psychology, I would need to put in at least another three years to finish an undergraduate degree, followed by a few years of graduate school and fieldwork.

Is it going to take me five years or more to make a respectable living? I was devastated.

With a pat on the back, Peter attempted to cheer me up, telling me, "Freddy, if you applied, you could probably get into the UC system." There may also be private schools that grant minority scholarships."

"The University of California?" I went from depressed to curious in thirty seconds.

"Sure. "Take, for example, Berkeley." He went on to say that the university was ranked among the top five in the country, but that it only accepted a small fraction of applicants. "But you never know."

Peter, the debate team's star and a tall, competitive athlete, was skilled at persuading, and he understood how to appeal to my yearning for a challenge.

"Berkeley, huh?" The name alone spoke to me.

As I pondered this news, I remembered my cousin Armando, who had grown up in Mexicali in the 1960s as a Harley-Davidson-riding intellectual. Armando was an enthusiastic reader and student of history who had followed the cultural revolution of the time, most of which had taken place at UC Berkeley. According to Armando, it was a magical place, and because of him, it was already a part of me.

UC Berkeley existed only in my imagination, far out of reach. Nonetheless, I chose to shoot high, as Tata Juan had advised. So I applied not only to Berkeley, but also to numerous other California undergraduate institutions. William & Mary was the only out-of-state college I applied to, primarily because Peter and his family told me it had a great debate program and granted scholarship support to some financially needy students.

I was taken aback when William & Mary sent me an admission letter and a hefty offer of financial aid. Had the admissions staff made a blunder? No way, Peter reassured me. I was fascinated by the pics of this lovely, centuries-old university campus. How could I refuse? Then I decided to do some study to determine Virginia's exact location. I'd overlooked a little detail: the school was on the other side of the nation, cutting me isolated from everyone I knew. The prospect of being separated from my family for months at a time was too much for me to bear. Instead, I was hoping to get into one of the UC institutions.

While I awaited their response, I set out to find new employment to help pay for the next part of my studies. My days as a welder and painter on the railroad were numbered. Given that the corporation charged its customers up to $500 per hour for my services, I should have been earning considerably more and receiving medical coverage and other perks, but my pay was set at ten dollars per hour. Benefits weren't a priority at the time, and I honestly thought my bosses paid me a fortune! After all, I'd been able to put myself through community college and assist my parents buy a house on that wage. The fundamental issue wasn't even discontent with the refurbishment of railway tankers. Simply put, it was time for a change. There were no realistic possibilities until Gabriel casually commented one day that I'd always been a poor man with expensive taste. True! I was lured to a beautiful boutique that sold imported designer apparel for males whenever I went to the nicer mall in downtown Stockton. Why not apply there instead? I was employed right away, ponytail and all!

I was too preoccupied with my hours at the store, track and field activities, and studying for my final semester of community college to be concerned about the status of my remaining college applications. I pretended, at least. I was literally on pins and needles! My entire family went through the process with me, and we were all overjoyed when the next-to-last response from Berkeley arrived-an acceptance letter! Ecstatic is too simple a word to convey my feelings. Though I couldn't believe the letter was real, I was pleased. The next day, an envelope with Stanford University's embossed return address and seal landed in our mailbox.

When my family came around to watch me open the Stanford package, I braced myself for a rejection, joking that my parents and siblings were overreacting and attempting to let us all down easy. Then I skimmed the first few paragraphs and skipped down to the verdict, took a little breather, then folded up the letter and returned it to the envelope. Everyone drew in close and attempted to provide consolation, assuring me that my rejection would be insignificant.

"Who cares what they think, anyway?" Gabriel asked, grabbing the envelope from my grasp and opening it himself. He shook his head when he noticed the response was yes. "You really had me fooled!" I was honoured to receive acceptance letters from two of my top choices, and I was much more pleased that everyone in my family could share in the accolades.

Now comes the difficult part. Which is better, Stanford or Berkeley? Stanford's tuition was far greater, which was a significant disadvantage. But, in the end, I chose Berkeley because of my cousin Armando, who had never even been there! Perhaps it wasn't the best decision. But, as always, once I made my decision, it was final. There will be no looking back.

Despite the fact that Berkeley is only an hour and a half away from Stockton, I was as unprepared for culture shock as if I had gone to Mars. The first indication that the university was not like community college was when I received my first test back in an anthropology subject.

I was shocked to see the grade at the top of my exam-a C!-as the teacher's aide came down the aisles matching names with tests and slowly handed them out. This cannot be right. I'd gone through the material backwards and forwards. My lecture notes from the professor were flawless. Were they trick questions, or what? Whatever had gone wrong, my heart sank.

"Did you study the Black Lightning lecture notes?" the TA inquired, seeing my surprise.

"Sorry?"

I discovered that these notes, created by teaching assistants for the classes they taught, were available for purchase in the university bookshops. Because TAs were frequently in charge of developing tests, students recognized that these notes would provide hints as to what would be on the test. I was grateful to get this insider information so early on-with enough time to perform well on subsequent tests and raise my grade in that class.

Eye-opening! I used to believe that mastering the content and immersing myself in the books would take me a long way and back. I realised that IQ was more than simply a book-based test; you had to be broad-minded and keep your ear to the ground for knowledge that could come from unexpected places. Brilliant book smarts were still a benefit, but so was the ability to plan your time, know who to ask for advice, and be aware of who was a trustworthy resource. This was an entirely new universe!

There was rarely a dull moment during my time at UC Berkeley. Though I began living on campus in a dorm and was fascinated by the assortment of exotic men and women who congregated in the living room of my suite and talked with a dazzling sophistication way above my head, I quickly moved into an apartment in Oakland, where I could study more easily and share expenses with a couple of guys who were experiencing the same culture shock I was. We might share notes on some of the strange events and characters on campus, such as the Hate Man and the Naked Man. The Hate Man, an equal opportunity hater, strolled around flicking the bird to everyone. He even proclaimed, "Hate is love." The Naked Man was dressed in nothing but his distinctive sandals and rucksack. Others soon followed in his footsteps. Many of these fans were persons who, to be honest, should not have been naked in public!

No matter how many times I saw those two or other unexpected sights on campus, I never grew accustomed to them. They reminded me that I was still a youngster from Palaco's outskirts. Indeed, by the end of the first semester, I was ready to return home and enjoy the holidays with my family. And I arrived just in time to work at the men's clothes business and replenish my diminishing bank account.

When I was flying through the mall on my way to work one day, I got a strange sense that something significant was going to happen. Not exactly a forewarning, but something along those lines. I looked up about an hour into the shift and saw a familiar face. Anna Peterson was browsing the display rack, clearly lost in contemplation.

A wonderful smile flashed across her face when she realised I was observing her. Seeing her emerald eyes again got to me. But, because we'd lost touch and had simply been passing acquaintances, I saw no reason to cherish romantic notions.

During our conversation, I heard that she was finishing up community college and had been accepted to the University of the Pacific in Stockton to pursue a teaching degree. When she asked how I liked Berkeley, I told her it was amazing but a little difficult. We ended our talk there, and she walked out of the store, ostensibly forever out of my life.

Not exactly. Anna happened to be in the mall later during the holiday and a few times throughout spring break and would pop by to say hello. Yamil, the manager of the clothes business, exclaimed after one of these trips, "That girl really likes you, Freddy!"

"You're crazy, you know that?"

"No," Yamil protested, and he reminded me that many people sought his counsel since he was a heart expert.

I respected his judgement because he didn't appear to be lying to me. When Anna came into the mall the next time, I greeted her with a little more flare than normal, asking, "How are you today, my lady?" I proposed after we discussed our plans for the rest of the school year. "Would you mind if I dropped you a letter from time to time while I'm away at Berkeley?"

"Not at all."

I was so excited that we might finally begin a courtship-albeit long-distance and over the mail-that I almost forgot to ask for her address. Fortunately, Yamil stepped forward with a pen and a pad of paper so she could record it.

And thus began a lovely correspondence. That day in the store, I finally began to put all the pieces together. It had almost been two years since she and her sister had approached me by the koi pond. I was starting to see the light thanks to the stars above.

I was also grateful to the anthropology TA for alerting me to the Black Lightning course materials. By studying them, I was able to not only ace my other courses, but also finish the year with an A- in that class. I joined my TA and a group of five students from the anthropological class in Caffe Strada, a popular meeting place in the centre of campus, feeling on top of the world with nothing but fantastic prospects ahead. We were there to celebrate the course's completion-and my improved grade! I typically avoided drinking coffee because I didn't need the extra energy, but this time I decided to indulge. Being at Caffe Strada-named after a Fellini film that I adored-and basking in the company of these colourful, intriguing people felt like a fairy tale to me. I felt quite fortunate when I considered my parents' sacrifices and the encouragement of others.

I wasn't shocked to hear the TA describe a rich upbringing with a private education, while the rest of my fellow students claimed hailing from a mix of privileged and middle-class households as we discussed the well-roasted coffee beans, foreign films, and our respective origins. The TA then asked, "And where are you from?"

"From Mexico". "You can't be from Mexico," the TA stated, looking me in the eyes. You're far too intelligent to be from Mexico."

An uneasy hush ensued. The topic of the conversation shifted. I said nothing but was relieved that the ruckus at Caffe Strada provided an excuse for me not to express my gut anger. Everything was heightened by the coffee rush coursing through my veins. But what I had just heard shocked me. I felt as if someone had cracked open my chest and pressed my heart into nothing, much like the day my cousin predicted I'd never leave the fields. This felt even worse. It was not about me. It was about my ancestors, my family, and my complete history. Years later, I recall the sensation of suffocation: my heart beating, my body numb, and my hands slick with sweat. "You're too smart to be from Mexico," was not the worst thing anyone had said to or to me. However, it triggered a flood of sad memories from my past. What made this any different?

Just as I later thanked my cousin for the kick that got me out of the fields, I'd look back and feel the same way about the TA's statement, which was more thoughtless and ignorant than malicious. However, the unpleasant truth that those statements showed at the moment was that I had no defence mechanism to counteract their impact. Because of who said them, they seeded seeds of guilt in me that grew into weeds and even twisted, thorny vines, confining me like a vise and making me desire to bury my past. I should have spoken or done something, and I'm not proud that the blow was delivered as a result of my weakness-my shame about who I was and where I came from.

I had a lot to learn before I could defeat the foe of insecurity. But I also utilised those statements to motivate myself and prove them wrong. That careless remark helped me mature, shed some naiveté, and become more serious in my focus. It served as a reminder that few people would have the opportunities I presently had. I owed it to myself and everyone who had faith in me to seize those opportunities, to make some decisions about my direction, and then to accelerate.

That was the objective I set for myself that day at Caffe Strada, sitting there, fuming but saying nothing.

6. Question the Rules and When Possible Make Your Own

What exactly is a miracle?

Healing is viewed as a type of miracle in medicine, but is it the only type? When I received a clear bill of health following a year-long AIDS worry, I certainly felt grateful, and I felt even more blessed when Anna told me that we had conceived our second child. My thirty-third birthday in 2001 was as amazing a celebration as I could have hoped for, with myself alive and thriving and my family healthy and growing.

Everyday miracles, similar to mine, occurred around me whenever a grim diagnosis was avoided or a patient was rescued from the jaws of death and was able to walk out of the hospital on his or her own two feet. But what about the patients who died as a result of their injuries or illnesses? Were their lives any less remarkable because of what they had done in the time they had been given and how they spent their final days? Was their power to impact others, their legacy for the living, the greatest miracle of all?

Early in my surgical residency and training at UCSF, as a midlevel resident, I saw the answer in the person of a little girl named Maria, who was brought into the paediatric department at Moffitt Hospital with what turned out to be a spinal cord tumour. This five-year-old child, who appeared to be from South America, had been abandoned, according to everything our Spanish-speaking hospital social workers could learn. She was small for her age, but she brought a fierce warrior spirit to her fight against the tumour that had rendered her paraplegic. When her bladder burst, she was unable to move or regulate her urination and other body functions, and she was taken into surgery. She had to have another surgery when she recovered from the first one to remove the tumour on her spinal cord.

Throughout the weeks she was with us, being cared for by three teams reporting to Pediatric Service-paediatric surgery, intensive care, and neurosurgery-I kept Maricela in my thoughts. A strange sense of déjà vu dogged me as I remembered my sister never receiving the medical care that could have saved her and my mother crying over the tiny casket amid an aura of misery that I couldn't comprehend. These recollections added to the grief of Maria's case and my anguish at witnessing her go through her tough path with no family to comfort her.

I stopped by her room between cases and sat with her, holding her hand and speaking to her in Spanish. As a doctor, I knew better than to underestimate the healing power of touch. Dr. Mitch Berger was extraordinary in this regard, as if the force and heat of his hand on a patient's shoulder or forehead could be transferred to that individual. Now I wanted to believe that Maria could be saved by healing energy. Despite our efforts to make her more comfortable, testing discovered another tumour, this time in her brain. The treatment choices ranged from further operations combined with chemotherapy and radiation to starting with chemo to see if we might buy her some time. But how humane would it be to prolong her life only to discover that we had also prolonged her agony?

The way Maria stared at me with her huge brown eyes, questioning, asking why, is what I remember most about her. Hers were the eyes of a very ancient soul, and I had the impression she realised she didn't have much time left. Maria appeared to be reassuring me as well. In other words, no. Her expression and actions indicated that she trusted us to take care of her and chose the best treatment for her. Maybe it was my imagination, but I got the impression she was urging us not to let her die anonymously and to make sure she was recognized when she left this world.

I went home the day Maria arrived at the hospital and poured my heart out to Anna. We ran together to check on our daughter, who was two and a half years old, healthy, safe, and loved, and we felt tremendously fortunate. All of the troubles and concerns about money, the long hours at work, and the lack of time to see each other vanished.

Anna and Gabbie approached me at the door when I came from work a day and a half later to suggest a plan. They'd gone out to get some modest gifts for Maria, intending to deliver them to her in the hospital. I was moved to tears by his words. We didn't have any money, and every cent that came in went toward rent and the little goods we could afford; we couldn't afford to dine at even the cheapest eateries. But Anna had used her budgeting skills to purchase these gifts. "What a beautiful thing you have done with your mom," I tried to convey to Gabbie, pointing out an unpleasant flaw in this selfless scheme. I'm quite proud of you. But guess what? There are laws prohibiting minors from visiting the hospital."

Her brow furrowed. Gabbie seemed to wonder how I could agree to such a stupid policy. Anna agreed with a shrug.

"OK," I responded, understanding I was no match for these two formidable women. "I'm popular among the nurses." Let me see whether they're willing to make an exception."

Anna was aware of my proclivity to query the rules from time to time. We were well aware that many institutional rules and regulations existed for a cause. But, in order to endure the furnace of my residency, I had to allow myself to challenge those regulations that did not serve the best interests of the patients or those in their service. Other, more humanitarian rules had to be applied in such circumstances.

I wanted to work my charm after being chosen by the nursing staff to obtain the Most Valuable Intern award during my first year. When I arrived at the paediatric nursing station the next day, I made a sweeping bow and asked the staff, "How are you today, my ladies?"

And what about my gentlemen?" Instead of asking if my wife and daughter may come in, I inquired when the ideal time would be for them to visit Maria. The nurses were initially apprehensive to accept the visit, but when Anna and Gabbie arrived with arms full of toys and cuddly animals, they waved us inside Maria's room. Gabbie made herself at home and began to offer the gifts to Maria, which Anna and I observed. My wife and I are still trying to put into words how it felt to see the two small children interact. The contrast in their lives and destinies could not be more pronounced. They were not at all different in the key aspects, and they became friends in an instant.

Maria did quite well from a combination of surgery and medicine that alleviated her severe symptoms throughout the month we observed her treatment. But none of these methods were adequate to eliminate the disease and stop its spread, and we realised she wouldn't be able to live the life we all wish for our children. Despite this, in her brief time with us, this young girl had become a star for everyone in the hospital as well as my family.

Maria was no longer in our care when she died; she was with a children's agency, which produced a report so that we could close the case and the paperwork. When I learnt that her battle was over, I needed to get some fresh air outside the hospital, which was something I didn't do very often. I stepped into a postcard-perfect spring day in San Francisco, with a blue, cloudless sky and the sun bouncing off the windows and spires of this great bay city. The weather was unconcerned with the solemnity of the occasion. There was nothing I could do to make sense of such a short life. We changed our approach to spinal cord tumour resection as a result of what we learned from Maria's case. Within a year, two young girls, ages three and twelve, were diagnosed with spinal cord tumours and benefited from this better resection technique. Both kids performed admirably and left our care with far fewer physical issues than we were accustomed to seeing. We all thought the outcome was a miracle for them and their families. While writing about our findings in a report that went through numerous drafts, I was reminded of the biggest miracle, Maria, the young girl who stood alone in the world and had left such an indelible impact. I held up the published article like a prize, thinking, Maria, this one's for you.

After surviving the first two years of training, I went into the third year expecting the "eating lightning and crapping thunder" part to be gone and the effort to be less. Wrong! I had merely been preparing for the championship fight. Now I'd see if I could silence those who said "you can't" and "who do you think you are?"

As in the final Rocky film, this aspect of my training would be about how much I could withstand rather than how powerfully I could deliver knockout strikes. As he says to his son, "It ain't about how hard you hit, it's about how hard you can get hit . . . how much you can take and keep moving forward." This would be my challenge: would I be able to stay in the fight after being hit and hit again and again?

Did I dispute the game's rules? Every time. I was sometimes thought to be going against the grain because I wasn't your normal neurosurgery resident. When others suggested that I was overstretching myself by performing research, working in laboratories, and training in the OR, I resisted even more. For example, I defied the prohibition on moonlighting. The requirement to support themselves and their families during their training did not offer a burden for many of the residents who came from wealthy homes. Questioning the rule became a necessity for some of us who had no other sources of income, so I chose to boost our money on weekends by working extra hours in out-of-the-way community hospitals. Geoff Manley, who was also married with children, had been in my shoes before and called these "power weekends."

For good reason, such outside work was frowned upon by higher-ups. But, for me, moonlighting was the only way to finance the high expense of living in San Francisco and put food on the table for my family. So I'd go out to my second job on Friday night and remain until six a.m. Monday, then return to UCSF to increase hours and responsibility.

Another example of violating the rules for me was refusing to let the pressure reduce my passion, interest, and amazement with the wonders of the human brain. Every day brought new reasons to marvel at the brain's talents, which science has just recently begun to comprehend. I began to see why Santiago Ramón y Cajal stated that before attempting to comprehend the cosmos, we must first investigate and uncover the secrets of the brain. We must become inner-space astronauts.

During this time, one notable procedure demonstrated how adaptable and robust our brains are. I was part of a team that removed a nearly six-centimetre-diameter brain tumour from a patient's frontal lobe. Given the size of the tumour and the possibility of collateral damage from this type of surgery, I was astounded to find the patient awake in the recovery room, fully conscious—a brightness in his eyes and a relief that he was home, safe and sound. He was flawless! He could have stood up and left the hospital right then. He was an inspirational example of how much a brain can survive and how effectively it can recover from even the most severe hits when he returned home two days later, with no change other than the elimination of a tomato-sized tumour that could have robbed him of himself.

There was a lot to learn about using the brain's innate ability to protect itself and fight sickness. Trying to digest the tremendous knowledge and skill that surrounded me was like drinking from a fire hose. Far too much! So the task was to discover a technique to metaphorically purse my lips and sip at the flow. The trick for me was to simplify everything at first, then progressively take in material in larger gulps. This unique method also assisted me in developing a focus for the research groups I was building with fellow residents and medical students, as well as allowing me to take the lead in collaborative writing projects with our lecturers. The groups were a mechanism for students to learn by teaching one another. These unconventional research teams grew as a result of Dr. Berger's leadership and the vision of a few of us, and they eventually became a more regular element of training.

Remembering that I was part of a team, as always, helped me soften the many sobering blows that seemed to come from every direction. Many of my fellow residents had been through similar fire experiences and emerged unscathed. We jokingly reminded one other that they didn't call it brain surgery for nothing. And we've all seen talented people fall by the wayside. One second-year resident forgot to put on scrubs in a certain professor's operating room and then made small chat with another resident while the professor was in the middle of handling someone's brain. The resident approached me after the operation and inquired if I believed he was in severe difficulty.

"No, no," I attempted to persuade myself, "everyone makes mistakes." Keep up the good work." When he went away, I turned to Nader Sanai, a medical student who would go on to become a neurosurgeon and scientist specialising on brain tumours, and said, "We'd better get the jam." That man is toast."

The resident in question had made other blunders as well, indicating that the mental and physical strains of training had impaired his judgement. He did, in fact, leave the program not long after. Every step ahead in this weeding-out process, like training for the Special Forces, was designed to make us doubt whether we had what it required to accomplish the unnatural job of brain surgery. After all, penetrating the inner sanctum of the cranium is not natural. It is significantly less intrusive to open up portals to other sections of the body. To get to the brain, however, we must either drill through the hard casing of the extremely protective human skull or uncover additional secret passages or side doors that will take us inside. Once inside, the main challenge is to complete our task while causing the least amount of collateral damage.

Despite the fact that this profession is unnatural, I found some parallels with my previous jobs that helped me grasp the necessary skills—from working on automobile engines as a child to welding and opening the lids of pressurised railway wagons. The wonderful sense of adventure in learning to chart the surgical route, however, was the most effective incentive. I began mentally planning the route of each brain operation from the time I saw the patient in the examination room. I learnt this technique from attending surgeons like Dr. Berger, who meticulously planned their combat strategy before entering the operating room—the door-die arena, where no manoeuvre could be left to chance.

Dr. Berger became more exacting as I grew stronger and more secure in my talents, making me question if he was trying to push me to my breaking point. But I now see that his tests were designed to show me that I could go further than I thought possible. While I bore the brunt of Dr. Berger's taskmaster side, every one of his patients benefited from his most devoted, compassionate healing side.

When I accompanied Dr. Berger to Moffitt Hospital to evaluate a pre-op patient who had been moved in for surgery from the maximum-security prison ward at San Francisco General, I learnt an important lesson in compassion. Inmates who required life-saving procedures were transported to Moffitt and held in a separate ward, where some were chained to the bedposts and armed guards were stationed outside each room. We referred to the inmates as "jailbirds" since they had temporarily escaped from the penitentiary to undergo treatment. Dr. Berger's patient that day was a large, muscular man covered with tattoos of swastikas, white nationalist insignia, and obscene inscriptions, including the words "Suck this!" and an arrow pointing to his genitals inscribed on his belly.

Mitch Berger's typical sympathetic bedside manner with this prisoner with the swastikas could have been overlooked because he was Jewish. Instead, Dr. Berger treated the patient with the same dignity, respect, and exemplary care that he did every other patient in that meeting and in the operating room.

This grace was seen in a variety of circumstances. He treated every patient the same, regardless of illness or prognosis, from the most famous to the most underserved. His example lives on in the practice I've developed every day. Nonetheless, I was perplexed for years about how rigorous my training had been under him. Dr. Berger realised that unless I was properly challenged-passing examinations that demonstrated I was the real deal-our field would never take me seriously. He would drive me harder if I drove myself. If a task was completed successfully, it could be improved. If I didn't perform to my full potential, others would conclude I was given preferential treatment because of my Mexican immigrant status. Regardless of how intrigued people were by my story-a magical fable about a migrant farm worker who rose via education-did they really want a former tomato picker removing tumours from their brains?

With Hispanic-Americans accounting for roughly half of California's population, I was the first Mexican-American to be trained at UCSF's neurosurgery department, and Dr. Berger recognized that many eyes would be watching to see how well I performed. He recognized that my sudden ascension into the spotlight would be distracting and perhaps dangerous to me. He also presumably expected people to make conclusions about me based on my ethnicity-and, yes, to ask whether I was clever enough or hardworking enough. He saw that I had similar potential-but only if I proved myself at the top level of ability-just as notable African-American neurosurgeons of previous eras had been able to break down barriers so that others may follow. He never directly mentioned any of these things to me. Dr. Berger, on the other hand, had instituted a program to teach inner-city kids about medicine earlier in his career, bringing them into classes at the Children's Hospital at the University of Washington, where he was the chief of Pediatric Neurosurgical Oncology. His goal was to train a new generation of neuroscientists from all walks of life.

Despite my analysis of Dr. Berger's ultimately altruistic goals, I couldn't speak to him without my voice rising an octave or two until I moved on to another school and became a faculty member in charge of educating residents myself! But by then, I'd learned so much from him that I was overjoyed when our paths crossed at a conference-and I told him so. Dr. Berger grinned and expressed his admiration for me. After we'd chatted about his work and mine for a bit, he leaned in to me and said, in his trademark Brando tone, "You know, Alfredo, the moment I decided to take you on, I knew you would be a leader and be able to do things that none of us could have accomplished." He then looked me in the eyes, put his hand on my shoulder, and said, "I know I was tough on you."

PART III BECOMING DR. Q

In December 2004, I, a young physician in my final year of residency in New England, after an overnight flight from San Francisco, was involved in a car accident while en route to Dartmouth from Boston's Logan Airport. I was considering a job offer from Dartmouth, despite having two other offers and the difficulty of getting permission to leave UCSF to interview. On the way, the town car I was sitting in slid on black ice and lost control, nearly colliding with another car. Both vehicles eventually came to a safe stop. This incident left a deep impression on my thoughts before he started his new job at Johns Hopkins. I realized that, no matter how much skill and knowledge one has, there are still things that are beyond one's control.

7. Hopkins

"Dr. Q, are you the attending neurosurgeon on call this weekend?", says the voice on the other end of the phone late on Friday, July 29, 2005.

Six years before, on my first night on call as an intern at San Francisco General Hospital, I had felt immense dread hearing identical words. The notion of evaluating a patient with a gunshot wound to the head had almost made me turn back as I walked down the stairs to the ER at the time.

But this time, a staff member in the emergency room at Johns Hopkins Hospital inquired whether I was the attending neurosurgeon on call. Not the resident or the surgeon in training, but the attending professor, the person in command in the event of a neurosurgical emergency! This new responsibility was both intriguing and intimidating, and I listened closely to the description of Mr. O's symptoms, who needed to be seen straight away.

I dashed into the stately corridor of Phipps, one of the oldest and most storied buildings on the Johns Hopkins Medical Campus, within minutes of hanging up the phone. I had planned to spend the entire month of August settling into my new position as an assistant professor of neurosurgery and oncology at the Johns Hopkins School of Medicine, and then to create my surgical practice and, eventually, a research laboratory from there.

I had no illusions about how simple this was going to be as the fourth-string quarterback in a department with three well-established and accomplished neurosurgeons. But then again, I was used to being the lowest man on the totem pole and having to prove myself! Or so I told myself as I dashed into the hospital, leaving the steamy Baltimore evening air behind and entering the chilly, air-conditioned hospital lobby as hundreds of visitors and personnel made their way to the exits, all ready to get home for a relaxing summer weekend.

I was hurrying down the corridor toward the emergency room when I came across a sight that would become a landmark for me: enormous mounted banners lining both sides of the hallway proclaiming Hopkins the number one hospital in the nation as rated by U.S. The magazine News & World Report. Not only this year, but year after year, poster after poster! Only time will tell if I had what it takes to hold my own at this establishment. But, in the meanwhile, I knew I'd come to the correct location if I wanted to play a meaningful role in the search for a cure for brain cancer.

Nonetheless, seeing those posters that first night on call was nerve-racking. Not that being afraid was a terrible thing. "If you're not afraid of failing, you'll never do the job," Cesar Chavez once said. If you're scared, you'll work like hell!"

I went to see Mr. O and his family, the echo of those words energising me. Starting with a very straightforward, clear-cut procedure is always preferred for any attending surgeon taking on their first professional case, much as boxers begin with the easier fights and work their way up to the championship rounds. As it turned out, once I'd studied Mr. O, I was in for a championship fight—a really difficult case.

Mr. O was a janitor at the University of Maryland who was about to retire when he abruptly stopped talking, had a seizure, and became unable to move his right leg or arm. When I asked him a question, he struggled to respond and could only mumble "Sorry" repeatedly. He could understand abstract ideas and had no loss of cognition, but he couldn't coordinate his voice cords and lips to make words. Because the brain tumour discovered during this visit had gone undetected for some time, it had grown to be so large and destructive that it was not only pressing on the part of his brain that controls speech and right-sided motor control, but it was also causing so much swelling that the normal plumbing channels that irrigate the brain were backing up and overflowing. So, aside from addressing the tumour, I knew we needed to operate within the next twenty-four hours to repair his brain's plumbing system. The tumour would then be removed.

We arranged the two portions of the operation for early the next morning, knowing that the surgery would take several hours to complete. I went over the details with Mr. O and his family, outlining the risks, discussing his fears, and outlining the potentially negative outcomes that are the realities of neurosurgery—from the possibility that neurological deficits would persist even after successful surgery to the possibility that he wouldn't wake up. But, in a pact that set a powerful precedent for me from then on, Mr. O and I agreed that when I met him in the OR in a little more than twelve hours, we would go in together as gladiators: he and I would combine our positive energy, working in partnership, each doing our best to achieve the best possible outcome.

"Deal?" I inquired. He struggled to say "Deal," as his children nodded stoically.

No matter how many brain surgeries I'd been a part of-opening, closing, or supporting the attending surgeon in all aspects of neurosurgery-everything changed for me on Saturday, July 30. I had rapidly assembled an amazing group thanks to Dr. Henry Brem, chair of our department. Because we were unfamiliar with one another, I spent additional time that early morning preparing my team members for every step in the two parts of the surgery so that we could move as quickly as a SWAT unit. I went into the operating room alone before everyone else and pictured where each of us needed to be, evaluating the layout and appraising the apparatus, machines, surgical tools, and equipment. I'd done this type of planning previously for other attending surgeons, but now I was doing it as the team's leader-a completely different experience.

Despite the fact that the second stage, tumour removal, would be the more difficult of the two, the first stage proved to be the more memorable because of the metamorphosis it created in me. None of my mentors had ever told me about coming into the OR for the first time as the general in command, no longer the second or third in command. Perhaps they hadn't mentioned it because the moment is so personal, a walk along the razor's edge of confidence and hubris. As the attending surgeon, you must summon superpowers for your patient while remembering that you are human and flawed. The key is to retain perfect serenity and control while summoning your highest levels of energy—a combination that allows you to bend time and space so forcefully that you could escape a speeding bullet like Keanu Reeves in The Matrix!

That morning, as I went to scrub at the sink outside the OR, I noticed a difference. I'd felt the stimulating effects of this practice many times during my training, but this time-and from now on-my senses took a quantum leap in intensity as I scrubbed furiously up and down each arm, getting the blood flowing, feeling my heart beat, and breathing faster. All distractions were washed away as I cleansed and dried my hands and arms with a sanitised towel. I was no longer the person I had been by the time I entered the OR, donned sterile surgical gloves, and ensured Mr. O was sterile-prepped. My tone of voice had changed. I hardly recognized the intensity and urgency in my eyes when I caught a glimpse of my face on a monitor. I realised time was of the essence the moment I cut through the skin, opened Mr. O's skull by drilling many small holes to remove the bone flap, and pulled back the dura, the velvet-textured covering of his brain. His mind was furiously dancing. The fluid that normally surrounds the brain was overwhelming the tissue because the tumour had blocked the drainage system; the brain was swelling rapidly, mushrooming with pressure at a perilous rate. While my resident continued to suction the blood, I cut a small hole in the plumbing system and, like if popping a balloon, was able to divert the water flow around the tumour; the swelling instantly began to subside. But there was a mess to clean up before we could fulfil our surgical goals in this first stage.

The Q Team won the first round. However, round two was a dogfight. Because of the tumour's massive size and entrenched nature-which, as expected, was a high-grade glioblastoma multiforme-and because it had embedded itself in the areas governing speech and motor control, I knew removing it would be a cruel, time-consuming task. We may have opted for an awake craniotomy if the tumour had been identified earlier (or symptoms had appeared), which would have allowed us to map the brain ahead of time and use Mr. O's answers to questions during surgery to lead us safely down the proper path. But, with his speech already fading, he had to be asleep, and I had to move in microscopic steps along a much more perilous path. Another source of concern was that, due to the increased frequency of seizures produced by the expansion of the big tumour, Mr. O. could seize during surgery, the tumour exploding under the touch of the scalpel like a buried landmine. The important trait required at this time, as exemplified by my mentors, was what some call the tiger's eye, the capacity to bring hyperfocus to what really matters in the OR—the patient—and to release one's skills to achieve the greatest possible outcome. For me, this meant moving around the brain in a neurosurgical dance that matched the patient's brain, orchestrating all the other moving parts of the operation, observing the big picture as well as the details, and communicating without words to ensure that everyone on the team was on the same page.

Dr. Michael Lawton had tutored me in the mystical arts of what I refer to as the astronaut chair-or "the throne," as others call it-for the last two years of my training at UCSF. The chair can truly save your life during long surgeries that can last eight hours or more. As you sit in the chair, tap your left toes to control the microscope's zoom in and out, as well as a specific pedal for modifying magnification; also, the left foot can move the microscope side to side, left to right, and up or down at an angle. The left foot must be partnered with the five functions it performs, such as the mouthpiece that moves the microscope in a circular motion and tilts it up or down. You manipulate two panels with your right foot that work with a mini welding machine to close up vessels and the like. Moving the right foot from side to side activates another pedal that works as an accelerator for suctioning extremely hard brain tumours. Meanwhile, as you sit on the chair, your hands are free to manipulate various controls for controlling the suction and welding equipment. The chair helps you to properly connect with your patient by allowing you to use all four extremities and your mouth. One incremental surgical manoeuvre may require you to use your entire body in the chair as you adjust the microscope, handle the brain, create an open space, go in with the scalpel in your right hand, and suction with the foot pedal and thumb force.

During the second stage of Mr. O's surgery, I considered how strong memory may be as a weapon in a life-or-death war. Mr. O's survival experiences had equipped him to combat the enemy; my memory kept pulling facts from the past to guide me when all avenues seemed barred and to provide insights into what might be on the other side of a structure in his brain. Memories of working on automobile engines as a boy, cutting weeds, operating tractors, scooping sulphur and scraping fish fat, mending and welding railway tanker lids—and finding out how to jump all types of fences—surfaced. Seeing Nana Maria excited by her work as a curandera, even after being on her feet all night, and envisioning how she lived, breathed, and became one with her patient provided some crucial data. Some of it came from stargazing on our roof on hot nights and fantasising about flying into space in my astronaut chair.

We did our janitorial work for Mr. O before closing, making sure we welded shut any small bleeders, contained any other oozing passageways, and left behind medications to prevent swelling and promote healing-along with a cancer-fighting chemotherapy wafer developed by Dr. Henry Brem, our Hopkins department head. With one last look around, I was pleased with the tumour excision, which had allowed us to retrieve everything we could see with our eyes and the microscope while leaving only the thinnest of outlines of where it had been. This thin layer kept us from accessing any of his brain's vital functions and served as a guide when we introduced medication to seal off the area, as well as acting as a firewall to block the aggressive cancer from returning to the same place.

The ultimate challenge for Mr. O was waking him up. No matter how well a surgery goes, whether or not patients wake up and how they wake up defines success or failure. No matter how many times I've gone to wake patients up after surgery, I still get nervous until they open their eyes. The most important test is if they can perform simple requests like squeezing my hand or holding up two fingers. Mr. O awoke readily, much to my delight, from my hand on his shoulder as I called his name. Even better, he greeted me right away, saying softly but firmly, "Hi, Dr. Q."

When I asked how he was feeling, he replied without hesitation, "Good." When will I be able to return home?" He could speak again!" His right-side movements have also returned. While this was an ideal ending and a good way to begin a championship-type case at Hopkins, Mr. O would face further fights. But what a heavyweight champion he turned out to be, battling with incredible grit for almost two years.

He fared so well at first that I almost convinced myself that we had permanently exiled the GBM. Periodic convulsions, however, began slowly and stubbornly, followed by a loss of control over his voice and muscle movements on the right side of his body. Mr. O had something vital to say to me the last time I saw him in my office, despite how difficult it was. He painstakingly explained what the wealth of the last two years meant to him. It soon became evident that he was comforting me!

I sat, my eyes watering, looking at his droopy face, his hair combed distinctly, wearing the Baltimore Ravens jacket that was his uniform, and I mourned for Mr. O. I wanted him to grow old, to see his grandchildren play, to take them on mountain hikes, and to have them sit by his bedside in his final hours.

He had, however, made his peace. For the majority of his life, he had gone to work and acted out of duty to feed and send his children to school, but he had been unable to realise how much they valued him. He seemed to be stating that the tumour was a gift that allowed him to feel and communicate how much he was loved. He told me everything over the following thirty minutes, word by word. He realised now that he had made a difference in his children's lives, and that they would miss him and cherish his memories. And he was the happiest he had ever been.

8. Gray Matter

Based on my experience of reaching terra firma at the hospital when I awoke after being rescued from the tank, I had a basic goal for my dream practice. I wanted to instill in my patients the same sense of security that I had. I had known that everything would be fine because of the doctor in the white coat's genuine concern and kindness. He was plainly a stranger, but there was something familiar about him. I believed he was from an immigrant or minority background, perhaps Hispanic, Indian, or Middle Eastern, based on his dark colouring and big nose and features, but his ethnicity wasn't the link for me. Rather, his caring demeanour and meticulous attention to my case made me feel like he could have been a member of my family, wanting the best medical care for me, keeping me overnight, setting up oxygen lines and intravenous infusions, and conducting a thorough assessment before releasing me.

I wanted patients to feel safe and grounded when they arrived at the modern, state-of-the-art clinic where my practice at Hopkins was headquartered, as well as that I would be a complete participant in the journey ahead, just as Nana Maria had been as a midwife. I couldn't think of anything more intimate than touching another person's brain, other than assisting a patient during childbirth.

Thinking of my patients as extended family, as well as the diverse array of staff, students, residents, nurses, technicians, and colleagues on the Q Team, I imagined a practice that was as welcoming and inclusive as the country that had given me terra firma on which to build a new life. With that in mind, I established an early policy requiring patients to have equal access to our office and to me at all times. I thought that the best way to accomplish this was to provide patients with my mobile phone number so that they or their family members could call me at any time, and to make my schedule available online to staff, residents, students, and colleagues alike. Many of my colleagues believed I was crazy. But why is this so? If I truly intended patients to be at the center of the practice-in the OR, clinic, school, and, later, laboratory-this seemed like a totally acceptable strategy to create the ambiance I envisioned of "mi casa es su casa."

A minor hiccup. While I could easily envision this welcoming, broad-based, highly diverse practice, the reality was that I had never created a practice before, as I had confessed to my wife when she recommended that if I built it, they would come. Neither did my second in command, Raven Morris, the physician's assistant I was lucky to have on my team from the start.

In fact, the procedure was so new to both of us that when I was told that I would be given a secretary, I had to ask Raven, "What does a secretary do?"

Raven, who had chosen to be a physician's assistant despite having the aptitude and drive to become a doctor and surgeon in her own right, didn't know either but spent no time in finding out. We were relieved to have someone to keep track of paperwork, plan appointments, and field calls, since we could now spend the majority of our time on patient care. Aha! Rather than constructing infrastructure and then waiting for patients to arrive, we could follow a much more organic process, with the practice evolving in response to the diverse requirements of the patients and their families.

Because I learned early in my training that tending to family members and loved ones is an important part of providing good patient care, we set up clinic hours that worked around people's schedules and made sure to create a direct line of communication during surgery from me to the loved ones waiting for the patient's life-or-death news.

When you're fighting for a patient to make it out of the OR alive, as was the case with RD, having family on hand can bring a lot of energy. RD died suddenly one day from what we assumed was a burst aneurysm. RD was in his early fifties, nearing the top of his professional career, otherwise in excellent health, happily married, and the father of three children. But, not long after getting at work that morning and speaking with coworkers, he began to shake with uncontrollable spasms before blacking out. A 911 call called paramedics, who came to find him comatose and intubated him, saving his life, before transporting him to the hospital. When RD arrived, he looked almost as bad as Nick Ferrando, whose sole sign of life had been a twitching finger.

When a person suffers from a brain aneurysm-a bulge in a blood vessel that can rupture violently and fatally-the chances of survival are slim. In general, one-third of people with aneurysms die before arriving at the hospital, another third die in the hospital despite heroic treatments, and only one-third survive. With the probability that RD had a burst aneurysm, I realized he had a two-thirds chance of not surviving. But if we didn't get to the bottom of the problem and fix it, the chances of him regaining consciousness were nil. I knew the stakes very well because of my training under Dr. Michael Lawton, who specialized in these types of severe cases-a career that would have been mine if I had stayed on at UCSF as his second in command.

I informed RD's family that the only way to save his life was to operate right away, but that if the problem was a ruptured aneurism, there was a 10 to 20% possibility that another rupture might occur, exploding like a grenade during operation. We proceeded with swift force after receiving permission from the family.

Because of the complications, I asked Dr. Olivi to join me in the operating room. Now that I'd been through a couple crises, the team understood me well enough to move with me, with minimal vocal directions from me. The same complete silence that I'd witnessed in my mentors' operating rooms was now in place in my OR, with only the sounds of monitoring equipment and drills as I began the craniotomy—using a blade capable of cutting through skin down to bone, carefully preserving every layer I removed, and then drilling a series of very small holes in the bone to enable me to remove part of it to make the opening, without putting pressure on the brain itself.

Following the removal of the bone flap, the dura was pulled back, which can be exceedingly tight, like the gripping petals of a Venus flytrap, and refuse to budge. Despite the fact that time was of the importance, I had to be careful not to peel the dura back too quickly, since this might disrupt the pressure in the brain and cause the pulse beat to speed up, go wild, or even halt, causing the patient's respiration to stop. None of these things happened. We also avoided the nightmarish scenario in which the brain rises like dough with too much yeast, requiring you to practically force the brain back down into the skull with both hands.

I adjusted the microscope into position after discovering merely a thin film of blood on RD's grey, pulsating brain. Dr. Olivi, my chief resident, the nurses, the anaesthetic team, the technicians monitoring the brain's electrical activity, students, and observers were all leaning in to see how quickly we might disperse any residual explosive or bulging vessels. With no symptoms of problems yet, everything peaceful and almost eerily normal, the vessel blew disastrously again the moment I detected the point of rupture, and blood spurted up like a geyser, splattering all over my mask, clouding my eyesight, and threatening disaster. But everyone fought back, and order was restored. Without saying much, the nurses went to work cleaning up around us, and Dr. Olivi worked as my eyes and extra set of hands, working alongside me until everything was back to normal. Then we were back on solid ground and clipped the aneurysm and made sure there were no more difficult spots before mopping up and leaving.

RD, who was still in a coma, had survived the worst of the storm, and we anticipated that he would recover after we moved him to the neuro-intensive care unit. He exhibited evidence of recovery in the first several days, voluntarily moving his arms and legs. But, without unexpectedly, his vessels contracted, stopping blood flow through them, and any progress we had made was undone. With everything that had happened to his brain since the first rupture, when he collapsed at work, it began to shut down, along with the key functions it regulated. The remainder of his body began to shut down, organ by organ-his heart, lungs, liver, everything. We tried a variety of drugs to help him recover, but we could only watch helplessly as his condition deteriorated.

After a month, when all possibilities had been explored and the findings of his neurological testing were so discouraging, I couldn't find a shred of good news to offer his family other than that I would be there for them and do anything they asked me to do. After several agonising sessions, they requested that care be removed, knowing that his chances of recovery were slim. I stayed with the family that day, and when they were ready, we went into the unit together, RD's wife on one side of the bed and me on the other. I held his hand while removing the feeding tube, followed by the breathing tube. His family members' faces, especially his wife's, were filled with sorrow and grace. He was gone in minutes, quietly and softly.

It wasn't the first time I'd been present at a patient's death, but it was the first time I'd suffered such a loss in my job as attending physician. It wouldn't be the last, of course. Dr. Michael McDermott was correct: it never gets easier. But, as physicians on the front lines of life and death, this is our reality. Every person who loses a patient handles the loss differently. For me, failure is difficult to quantify, a bitter pill to swallow after so many twists and turns in a patient's journey-when all efforts to restore them to safety and health are futile. But being present with a patient at the end to provide care, to provide such consolation as one human being can give to another, is also an honour and a gift. I remember seeing RD's light in the minutes before and after he died. I'd seen this light before with other dying people and would do it again. I'm not sure if it's my imagination or the way the daylight fills the room at those times, but I believe that the wonderful life energy that exists in all of us has a kind of brightness that may be seen at the time of death. There's no better way to describe it than that, except to say that the light is larger than life, and perhaps it's there at the end of the passageway between this life and the next to let us glimpse the great hereafter, whatever it truly is, at the moment when people go peacefully to sleep for the last time. Seeing that light and the expression of peace on RD's face, I realized we had grown close in the month he had been in my care as a fellow soldier, and I was heartbroken to see him go.

Every physician and health care worker must develop his or her own way of coping with a patient's death, just as each of us must follow our own route when grieving the loss of a loved one. The nursing staff, who offer hands-on care to patients around the clock and experience the toll that a loved one's illness takes on family members, understand this well. I've often assumed that if most of us who deal with loss on a daily basis didn't have some type of post-traumatic stress disorder, something was wrong with us. Those of us who choose not to remove ourselves and compartmentalize our feelings require an avenue to process the experience, whether through therapy, attending a patient's burial, creating a personal grieving ritual, or all of the above. Something that helps me and is meaningful with RD is to slow down, take as long a break as I can, and maybe take a stroll outside to gaze at the world the patient has left behind and appreciate the life he or she lived.

Whether I'm outside or walking from the hospital back to my office along the basement route, everything seems quiet and empty, and the quality of the light in the atmosphere is dimmed somehow by the loss of that patient, that person, who is no longer a part of my life and the world. As I decompress, the best way to rekindle my fire is to realize that I'm not superhuman; like anybody else, I can only work harder and use my knowledge and passion-and inspire my students to do the same-to attempt to make a difference for those in need.

It is human nature to remember incidents that did not end well rather than those that did. The reality is that the vast majority of the over 300 procedures I currently perform in a year go exceedingly well. And, even if the war is eventually lost in cases of brain cancer, the majority of patients have better-than-expected results. Nonetheless, we surgeons have a tendency to recall where we fell short, when nature dragged us and our patients to our knees. But I've never tried to numb my feelings of grief when a patient dies; instead, I use these losses as motivation to perform better and fight harder in memory of the patients who didn't make it.

Strange as it may appear, a patient's death reminds me how much I like what I do, lest I forget that not long ago I was picking tomatoes in the fields and now have the unusual opportunity of treating and handling the human brain. To earn the trust and faith of people, I must also remember that what I do is fraught with danger. So, in addition to my walks, my remedy, today as much as in the early days of my profession, is to love all aspects of what I do, even the most difficult portions of the job, and to look for the joy that can arise even in the darkest of times.

9. Seeing the Light

"There's a Professor Schmidek on the line for you," the Hopkins hospital operator said as I took up the phone in my office after rounds one Sunday evening.

"Did you say Schmidek, as in Dr. Henry Schmidek?" I inquired, confident that I didn't know anyone by that name other than

Professor Schmidek, whom I had met at Dartmouth a year before. He was a legendary personality in science and medicine, as well as the editor of Schmidek and Sweet's Operative Neurosurgical Techniques, the world's most extensively used text in neurosurgery. "Please, yes, thank you, put him through!"

A brief flashback to my winter vacation to New Hampshire brought back memories of the heart-stopping slide on the black ice and my lingering question about why I'd been obliged to go. Already feeling the draw of Hopkins, I should have realized that no matter how impressed I was with Dartmouth, my path would not change. On the other hand, I wouldn't have missed seeing Professor Schmidek and spent two unforgettable hours discussing everything from neuroscience to parenting.

I had no idea why he had called me now, but I was happy to hear Dr. Schmidek's booming voice inquire, "Alfredo, how are you doing?"

"Everything is going swimmingly. Thank you very much! I hope everything is well with you, Professor?"

"Well, very well."

I was flattered that he had interrupted his busy schedule for a social call to see how I was enjoying Baltimore, so I was astonished when he abruptly changed the subject, stating, "There is something I want to talk to you about." He took a breather. "It will transform your career." "Do you have a few moments?"

Naturally, I did!

Dr. Schmidek's normally upbeat demeanor took on a more solemn tone. "Alfredo," he said at that point, "this next edition of Schmidek and Sweet's will be my most ambitious and my last."

"But you're a young man," I pointed out, wondering why he was so sure he could say everything in the five years or so it would take to produce the next version. New techniques in our profession were being developed on a daily basis, and laboratory discoveries were also changing the direction of neurosurgery.

Schmidek did not elaborate on his reasons, other than to remark that future editions would need to be written by the next generation of professionals. "Like you, your colleagues, residents and students," he went on to say.

I was perplexed. Although the following generation may contribute, why would he step aside as editor after his sixth edition?

"Good," replied Dr. Schmidek. "I look forward to working with you." "I'd like you to help me edit my next and final edition of Schmidek and Sweet's," he explained, astonished by my silence.

Given the numerous more knowledgeable and recognized authorities he could have consulted, I was astounded. Why me? But I mumbled something about what an honour this was and how excited I was even by the thought.

"Wonderful!" Dr. Schmidek said before signing off. "We'll be in touch."

After hanging up the phone, I attempted to tell myself that this was no big problem. What was I thinking? This was incredible! And after mentally replaying the conversation a few times, I realised that, aside from the fact that this chance would revolutionise my career, the question of why I had needed to travel to Dartmouth was finally solved.

Everything made sense, even my emergence from the ice crash. Not only was I supposed to meet Dr. Schmidek, but I also needed to review old Tata Juan classes.

Now I understood why my grandfather took us on treacherous roads that could have sent us crashing over the cliffs at any turn; why he stopped periodically to explore caves and look at other landmarks that weren't always of interest to an impatient little boy. Now I saw why our hikes carried us off the main path and into the woods, offering no immediate results other than a sense of discomfort. Those detours and hazards were all part of the journey, all part of the eventual achievement of reaching the summit, all part of teaching me to trust my own instincts in the future.

Professor Schmidek and I started working together immediately after he phoned, talking on the phone at least once a week and sending material to each other on a regular basis—even though I wasn't helping in any official role as a co editor or contributor. Although Dr. Schmidek was spending the year at Oxford University in England, we ramped up the pace in the fall of 2008, expecting to create a clear overview of the massive job by Christmas.

But all changed in October when I learned that Henry Schmidek had died unexpectedly after a heart attack. He had only been 71 years old. Our sport has lost one of its most colourful and youthful figures. I was saddened for his family, but I was also disappointed that he had been unable to accomplish the project that had been so important to him. I figured the project had been terminated or needed a new head editor.

Then, a month after his death, I got a phone call on a weekend at home from Mary Schmidek, who wanted to talk about the future of the project I had been working on with her husband.

"I understand," I answered, expecting she was about to tell me that the editing would be handed over to more established, experienced hands.

Mary, on the other hand, stated that her husband, evidently feeling that he might not live to see the publication of his final and most ambitious edition, had asked me to be the lead editor of Schmidek and Sweet's Operative Neurosurgical Techniques' sixth edition.

I was at a loss for words. The honour and responsibility were both humbling. Mary Schmidek informed me that her husband had excellent intuition and knew that I would approach the work with the same enthusiasm and adventure that characterised his life. She went on to discuss his lifelong fascination with the outdoors. Dr. Schmidek, in addition to achieving national records in sailboat racing after only two years of participation and enjoying fly-fishing, had recently discovered a taste for driving his off-road vehicle at high speeds.

I discovered then that there are various types of off-roading, some planned and some unplanned. I was more grateful than ever that I'd taken the trip to Dartmouth four years before.

After Mary and I had said our goodbyes, I went to the computer and opened the last file I'd provided to Dr. Schmidek, picking up where we had left off a month before. The sixth edition of Schmidek and Sweet's Operative Neurosurgical Techniques is nearing completion and is scheduled for publication in early 2012.

Meanwhile, Anna and the kids decided to prepare a special supper to commemorate my new assignment, which would require some more work at home over the following four years but also introduce us all to new colleagues and friends from all over the world. The many volumes of this encyclopaedic style would also connect me to leading research being done in the quest to cure brain cancer, with contributions from prominent neurosurgeons at all the top institutions in the United States and other countries.

I was appreciative of everything as I looked around the table at my cherished family, sure that I had lived up to my nickname of Lucky Quinones. To be sure, the last three and a half years at Hopkins had presented us with fresh challenges. My lengthy hours did not make

Anna's transition to living in Baltimore any easier in the first year or so, before the practice began to truly rock 'n' roll. And now that everything was moving at a faster pace, the long hours just kept coming, leaving her to hold down the fort with three very busy children (and a burgeoning cat population).

But, in some ways, our efforts were finally bearing fruit. Anna's creative and budgetary abilities were showcased in our home, which was a dream come true for us. We were even talking about putting up a pool in the backyard because all three of our children are natural swimmers like their mother. Still, if we were to benefit from Tata Juan's teachings, perhaps it was time to break free from old habits. To that end, Anna suggested that now that my practice was up and running, we look at my calendar together and set out at least one night a week when I would be home for dinner, as well as the best part of one day on the weekend for me to enjoy being a family man.

Sometimes a simple, little step works wonders. Though the new schedule was far from ideal, Anna and I were able to sneak in a date night every now and then, much to everyone's surprise. What a treat to go out for dinner and a movie. We had come a long way to get here.

Now that the kids were older, I was thrilled that they could go to Hopkins with Anna on occasion (following in the footsteps of Walter Dandy, whose children famously walked the hallways of Hopkins in his day). Most of our visits were simple to arrange, except for the time I enthusiastically suggested to my wife that she bring the kids to a lunch I was throwing for the nursing staff and a few members of my team—including my two physician's assistants, Raven Morris and Jill Anderson, who were a fantastic addition to our group. "About this lunch on March tenth... um, you forgot, didn't you?" Anna called as soon as I sent it out.

Oh my goodness! Her birthday is the 10th of March! I'd been doing so great, but now I'd forgotten. I went back into the doghouse!

For many years, I believe Anna and I both expected to reach a point when there would be more time for us—a true separation of business and home life. We were both coming to terms with the fact that this was always going to be a work in progress by this point. We were aware that others were struggling with the issue of balance, and that no one, to our knowledge, had an answer that we did not.

Anna, of course, never used my demands as an excuse to withdraw her love or support, nor did it stop her from getting progressively involved in various elements of my job at Hopkins—adding new responsibilities to her role as chief counsel in all my decisions. Anna had started an annual Thanksgiving tradition of preparing an excellent feast and having an open house for our ever-expanding extended family of students, residents, grad students, postdocs, and patients a few years ago. Members of the team that do research in the laboratory that I was eventually able to establish at the end of 2007 are frequent guests at our yearly fiesta. Anna, in fact, deserves credit for a concept that became one of the lab's secrets to success.

Initially, the Neurosurgery Brain Tumour Stem Cell Laboratory, later known as "Dr. "Q's Lab" had the smallest of armies—just me and researcher Grettel Zamora, a recent Hopkins biology graduate. We assigned ourselves a two-pronged challenge: first, to connect the dots in our understanding of how brain tumour cells travel through and invade normal brain tissue, and second, to find medicines to stop the invasion and eventually eradicate the invaders.

In establishing our approach, I was inspired by my hero, Santiago Ramón y Cajal, who emphasised the need of simplicity in investigative scientist work. Cajal also cautioned scientists not to be excessively constrained by established science or the legendary geniuses who founded it.

My lab was also impacted by another of my heroes, Dr. Ed Kravitz's love for research. He may retire at any time with a tremendous corpus of work, including his study of the primordial neural battlegrounds of various species. But he keeps pushing the envelope, most recently investigating the inner workings of fruit flies and how their level of aggression influences how they live and die. Ed refers to this initiative as the Fruit Fly Fight Club.

Because of these influences, I have kept with the most basic, albeit unconventional, method of explaining the stakes of the battle against brain cancer. Assume we simplify the explanation such that even a young child from the fringes of a small town called Palaco in Mexico can understand the difficulties. We've compared a cancerous brain tumour to a mythological serial-killer dragon in earlier descriptions: if you chop off its head, it develops two more heads and summons additional deadly cohorts to join the battle. My story continues, the boy dragon slayer began with nothing more than a handcrafted stick to track and fight the monster. But, as the dragon grew stronger, the child grew stronger as well, developing a few clever weapons to add to his armoury. And, in his most significant move, the youngster gathered a small but superb army to fight beside him.

So, what is this dragon's face like? We know that over 600,000 people in the United States, including approximately 30,000 children, are living with a primary brain or central nervous system tumour. Every day, ten children are diagnosed with paediatric brain tumours, totaling about 3,700 per year. Approximately 75 percent of non adult brain tumour patients are under the age of fifteen. Brain cancer is the deadliest kind of childhood cancer, and even noncancerous tumours can be fatal, especially for youngsters, if the tumour's position makes surgery or medicinal therapy impossible.

We also know there are more than 130 forms of brain tumours, which can make identifying brain cancer a challenge. Gliomas—a range of low- to high-grade tumours—are the most prevalent type of primary brain tumour. Some 124,000 people in the United States have malignant brain cancer, and each year nearly 14,000 individuals in the country die of the condition. Around the world, the number of brain cancer deaths per year is between 130,000 and 140,000. The disease is a mass murderer by any standard.

The biggest killer among the glioma tumours, the high-grade glioblastoma multiforme (GBM), infiltrates the healthy brain with its deadly cells so as to make total surgical removal practically difficult, which in turn permits it to come again in 99 percent of instances. Even with a combination of chemotherapy and radiation treatment, median survival remains at little over one year for patients with GBMs. We have learnt that the tumour likely acquires its first foothold in a specific population of cells that share features with normal neural stem cells and brain tumour stem cells. The worrying discovery is that the cells that create the tumour cells can regenerate, are not prevented by present therapies, and can move large distances.

When Grettel and I began our study in the lab, our first step was to apply existing information about how normal stem cells in the brain move to our own findings of how tumour cells behave. The immense hurdles of the mission we had set for ourselves became clear almost immediately. The first terrible conclusion was that with only the two of us, our efforts would take considerably longer than the time remaining for our brain cancer patients. We wanted to expand and broaden our army, bringing in experts from many fields to cover all battle stations. But how do you do it? How could I inspire more students from the school of medicine and other scientific departments, as well as residents, graduate students, and postdocs, to not only undertake revolutionary research in the lab but also to feel the same feeling of urgency that we neurosurgeons do in the OR? How could I persuade team members to give up one of their very busy nights to attend a weekly meeting to exchange findings—and thereby keep the collaboration and competition alive? The most pressing question was how I would persuade these amazing young minds from every corner of the globe and every cross-section of society, as I envisioned, that I had something valuable to contribute to the conversation and the lab.

Anna provided the answer. She reminded me of the lean days of my residency, when a rare night out entailed one cheeseburger for our kid and none for us at a fast-food restaurant. If I added refreshments on the agenda, perhaps some researchers might attend meetings. I accepted her concept and ran with it, adding my own simple embellishments: first, set up a not-to-be-missed Friday night meeting, planned for the end of the week when researchers' brains are already exhausted and they need a dinner break; second, offer them an appetising meal with plenty of portions. They'll believe everything I say and think I'm a genius when they're already drowsy and half asleep—postprandial and lulled into complacency by their full stomachs!

Despite this brilliant strategy, an almost insurmountable obstacle remained: financing. Money would be required to initiate the research, pay the researchers, and cover the significant costs of constructing the business I had in mind. I applied for a dozen grants without knowing how difficult this effort would be—a perfect example of ignorance being bliss. True to habit, I felt I might as well aim high, so I targeted the most sought-after and prestigious grantors, devoting countless hours and effort to filling out the forms. Even though I was optimistic, I was taken aback when seven of the twelve grants were approved—from prestigious organisations such as the Howard Hughes Medical Institute, the Robert Wood Johnson Foundation, and the National Institutes of Health. We quickly found, with a growing team and now with money, that the availability of human brain tissue, particularly brain tumour tissue, was critically limited. I'd seen most of that tissue carried away for disposal in surgery after operation, after removing innumerable tumours; only a tiny quantity wound up on a slide for pathology. My colleagues and I devised a simple solution. Why not give them the option of donating any intraoperative tissue to our lab? To our surprise, practically every patient not only agreed to provide this incalculably vital gift to our study, but did so with such zeal that it inspired the establishment of our lab's tissue bank. The bank contains cancer and noncancer specimens from adult and paediatric patients, as well as tissue that would otherwise be wasted following surgery. Our lab also contains a collection of postmortem brain tissue, with over 700 specimens gathered as of this writing.

Patients and their families consistently tell us that being able to donate to the tissue bank and the lab's work offers them hope and a feeling of purpose, and helps them to be a part of something bigger than their individual challenges.

So, how did it all work out with increased funding to improve the lab's infrastructure and the establishment of the tissue bank, which is critical to establishing cell cultures and cell lines for use in our investigations and those of other scientists conducting critical research? We soon had about two dozen team members who were fully invested. The Friday night meetings quickly became standing-room-only occurrences.

The sessions, which are open to the entire Hopkins community, the general public, and the media, draw enormous numbers in part because of what's on the menu—every cuisine from Chinese to Indian, soul food to deli, Mexican, Italian, Peruvian, and more. I have to remind researchers to arrive early so they can go through the buffet line before it runs out. The major lure for the sessions, however, is the presence of guest speakers. Our stars are our patients, who are scientists in their own right and offer the necessary sense of urgency for our study.

This perspective on the crucial role of patients was discussed with my friend and lifelong mentor Dr. Esteban González Burchard, who was on campus in mid-2008 as an invited distinguished professor and found time in his schedule to attend a Friday night meeting.

"You know, Fredo, you are the only person I know who would spend all day in the OR on a Friday and then, when everyone else is knocking off early, you're throwing a meeting," Esteban commented as we sprinted across the Hopkins campus toward the laboratory. That's dedication!"Then he added, "And insane!""

Fortunately, I responded, there were other mad researchers eager to join me.

"How do you get your employees to stay late on Fridays doing science?" Not everyone is as determined as you are."

The solution was straightforward. "I've had the good fortune to live the American dream, to seize opportunities." If somebody wants to join my team and work hard, I will provide them with even more opportunities."

Esteban wondered whether they were inspired by my decision to reject large sums of money given elsewhere in order to pursue the ideals I believed in. He said, "They can relate to you as a guy who drives a Honda SUV instead of a BMW."

True, many of the researchers enjoyed my anecdotes about making the most of what little I had, such as the saga of my red pickup truck's customised hydraulic kit, which allowed me to lift and lower it to Whitesnake songs! But I also had other sneaky ways of provoking the members of my team. I was not above, for example, calling a lead researcher at 6:00 a.m. on a Sunday morning to see how his or her experiment was doing.

Then we'd talk over some great ideas I had for a paper that I was confident the researcher would want to write up. Motivation!

Esteban burst out laughing. He was well aware that the mentors who had inspired me, including him, had influenced my style as a mentor.

He appeared to detect the atmosphere when he and I arrived in time for supper before the conference, especially among the excited and worried lab scientists who were slated to discuss their results that night. But it wasn't until I brought the meeting to order and introduced our guests, Ken and Betty Zabel, that I noticed my good colleague's eyes light up.

Ken, my brain cancer patient, began by telling everyone how delighted he was to tour the lab and observe the team's dedication.

"He works for us!"" I jokingly said, forcing Esteban to shake his head at the well-worn statement.

Ken and Betty both laughed. Ken, a huge, gregarious, and very spiritual guy in his early sixties, claimed that he could keep his spirits up because he thought that everything that happened to him was part of a larger purpose. "God has a plan," Ken declared, and he explained that he believed that part of that purpose included helping to find a cure for brain cancer.

Ken then told us his narrative of realising the American dream after developing a successful firm from the ground up, with staples still visible on his bald head after his recent craniotomy. He and Betty had been married for twenty-five years, their second marriage. They'd merged their two families into one big family and had never stopped acting like newlyweds.

"I was so lucky to meet Betty," Ken said. "She was a beauty, and I was this big bald guy," he remarked, adding that he had never had to modify his haircut for brain surgery.

Betty chimed in, saying that their romance was love at first sight, bald head and all. She also stated that Ken had always been concerned about his health; he ate a balanced diet, exercised, and had received annual checkups and tests for years with the hope of living a long, healthy life. But, while abroad on business one Friday afternoon, he arrived at the local hospital with peculiar symptoms.

Doctors informed him that his brain was infected with cancer and that he needed surgery on Monday. However, Ken felt pressured into something that wasn't appropriate. He remembered lying in his hospital bed in Florida, holding his BlackBerry, and felt God's hand instructing him to explore the Internet to learn more about his alternatives. While looking for the best neurosurgeon hospitals and keywords concerning promising brain cancer research, he came upon a link to a story about Johns Hopkins and "Dr. Q's Lab."

Ken dialled the Baltimore directory assistance number and was eventually connected to a secretary in the neurosurgery department, who gave him my office number. He mentioned in a phone message that he was supposed to be my patient and that a copy of his MRI should already be there. He went on to say that he needed to be seen right soon.

At the lab meeting, I saw a lot of mouths drop and eyebrows raise. "What did you do after that?""Someone inquired.

I rushed in, remembering how confused I was when I learnt of the message from Ken Zabel who lived in Florida and for whom I had no records. However, if films were lost or a patient in need was unable to see me, someone had to take care of the problem. So I dialled his number.

"I couldn't believe Dr. Q picked up the phone and called me," Ken said to our small group. In truth, he wasn't sure his ruse would work. Ken said, "No matter what happened, I just knew this was the guy I was supposed to see."

How could anyone refuse someone who made that much effort? I informed him that if he could make it to my office on Monday, I would be delighted to meet him.

Ken Zabel's case was truly grave. We were able to execute an awake craniotomy and buy him some time because he still had all of his linguistic and cognitive faculties. As everyone in our lab meeting could see, he had done an excellent job. But there was at least one more tumour in a different part of his brain, and another surgery was very certainly in need. Worse, the serial murderer we knew GBM to be—and had seen under the microscope and in experiments with the tissue Ken had provided to the lab—was far from dead.

At this point, Esteban merely nodded his head, indicating that he now understood why I attempted to engage my team's emotional energies as he glanced around the room and saw how emotionally linked everyone was to the situation of this real-life patient sitting there with his wife.

But I don't think any of our guests were prepared for the uproar that ensued as the night's presenters took turns reviewing their latest discoveries. The atmosphere during these weekly presentations frequently takes on the intensity of a CSI: Miami or House episode, with everyone in the room channelling their inner Sherlock Holmes. The sense of urgency was evident in the room that night, as if everyone understood a murderer was ready to strike and knew we needed to pool our resources to assist one another with existing investigations. This was not the moment to comfort Ken and Betty. Our mission was to present genuine discoveries and legitimate causes for optimism.

I expected our visitors to be fatigued and ready to say good night by the conclusion of the discussion, when we had gone into very difficult neurobiology. I assumed that after three presentations-two in PowerPoint and one in the form of a minidocumentary-our lab staff would be eager to get home and start their weekends. Not so. I watched with paternal pride as all the researchers approached the Zabels and Dr. Burchard introduced themselves-a moment unlike any Esteban had ever experienced, he later told me.

His reply underlined for me that our method was breaking down barriers and promoting collaboration, due in part to patients and families like the Zabels, who contributed not only their words and emotion but also tissue taken during surgery. The minidocumentary we watched that night revealed cellular activity in tissue from Ken Zabel's tumour. We noticed dramatic activity on a tissue slide using sped-up film technology, demonstrating the multiplication of cancer cells. This research was not only promising, but it was also moving at a rapid pace-because there was someone on the team whom everyone now knew personally and whose life was in danger.

Ken Zabel's battle was far from done. While I'm not convinced that everything happens for a reason, I can believe that if we investigate the mysteries of our lives, the solutions will help us find our life's purpose. The work's direction and the atmosphere at the lab certainly make me feel that way. I remember getting chills when one of our neuroscience postdocs, Hugo Guerrero-Cázares ("Guerrero," which means "warrior"), presented his findings, reminding us that these migrating cells could be "the missing link" in unravelling the murder mystery of brain cancer, eventually showing us how to stop the most lethal tumours in their tracks and one day even revealing how to prevent them from growing at all.

I've been dubbed not only crazy for believing such answers are within our grasp, but also naive. Embracing hope, on the other hand, strikes me as neither naive nor unreasonable. Many of the life-saving medical remedies that we now take for granted were developed by people and teams that were similarly optimistic. Every day, I encounter patients who know they will die yet choose optimism over despair. Many do so in order to appreciate every last second of their lives. Others find solace in contributing to science and making a little contribution to history. They take solace in the knowledge that what we learn from their suffering will aid in the prevention and treatment of diseases in others.

As the principal conductor of Dr. In Q's Lab's orchestra, I not only get to organise, encourage, and coordinate investigations, but I also get to be an instrumentalist-a researcher alongside members of smaller, two- to four-person teams. After only three and a half years, the lab has become a solid foundation where bright minds may feel comfortable and empowered in their work, with my encouragement and belief that they are about to discover something significant.

One group of four researchers, for example, is investigating a promising new technique for treating GBMs that employs adipose-derived (yes, fat!) mesenchymal stem cells, which have been found to move to tumours. These stem cells can be coaxed to release anticancer genes or proteins by genetic manipulation. The lab has developed a malignant tumour model that mimics the lethal characteristics of glioblastoma, as well as cutting-edge technologies for tracking cellular migration in real time, which can be caught on MRIs. We are so satisfied with the results of the controlled tests that we intend to apply this therapy to patients with brain and other tumours.

Another team is starting work on the "recruitment hypothesis." Because we know that removing a GBM does not eradicate cancer and leaves micrometastases behind, this team will investigate how normal neural stem cells move and what happens to them when they undergo changes that make them resistant to therapies. If the daily analogy is that one bad apple ruins the whole bunch, then we seek to find the signalling pathway that connects cancer stem cells and normal neural stem cells and create methods to disrupt their communication systems. These nasty cells are extremely intelligent, and our task is to outwit them.

I play cheerleader, teacher, student, and devil's advocate during Friday meetings, poking holes in ideas or promoting healthy debate and collaboration. Even if a presenter explains a scientific concept that seems great in principle, it is my obligation to ask why current therapies aren't effective in curing brain cancer. Such hurdles might spark "aha" moments or point up areas that need more investigation. One interesting lab study is looking at how radiation impacts stem cells that are seeking to migrate from the primary part of the brain where they live. The experiment intends to demonstrate how radiation may affect progenitor cells to participate in the promotion of healthy stem cells in order to get a better knowledge of both progenitor cells and stem cells. Clinical studies, we hope, will begin soon. This research will assist clinicians in accurately targeting radiation doses and determining effective dose levels; ideally, it will find molecular and pharmaceutical substances for treatments that will boost progenitor cell survival and improve these cells' migratory capacities.

With all of these clever weaponry, one of our main concerns in our discussions is how to keep one step ahead of our assassin. Since we know that GBMs thrive in low oxygen environments with enhanced glycolic activity, we're wondering if lowering oxygen levels and regulating glucose metabolism will slow tumour growth.

Our mine team of researchers used the tumour model from donated tissue to replicate tumour growth in an experiment exploring Robo receptor cells and Slit proteins (a family of chemo-resistant proteins). This vital study is akin to deciphering the killer's language, which leads tumour stem cells to infiltrate the brain.

When answers aren't forthcoming, I turn to the power of simplicity again and again. This does not imply that I am looking for an easy explanation or a silver bullet answer. Because the causes of brain cancer are multifaceted, so should the treatment and techniques of halting the disease. But, as I learned from Tata Juan and the fateful (or inadvertent) meeting I had with Professor Schmidek at Dartmouth, big things happen when you put in the effort, trust your intuition, and allow your imagination to run wild.

If I needed any proof of that view, I discovered it at our lab meeting one Friday night, like any other Friday night. I had just finished a second case in the OR and had collected tissue to go to the lab with me, enjoying our capacity to immortalise our patients and make them part of our team as usual.

We went down to work after a fantastic Middle Eastern buffet, and the jovial atmosphere quickly turned to a serious one.

Tomás Garzón-Muvdi, MD, MS, one of our research fellows, was going to deliver papers on which he had been working hard.

The talk may have gone a little differently. But Tomás was correct. We all saw the light and realized that a transformational hint had been discovered, one that we had been looking for for three years, this breakthrough coming only after a series of experiments that came one after the other. Big stuff was going on!

There are various reasons why I enjoy what I do, but one of the most important is the ability to gain "perspective on life's values," as one of my patients, Adrian Robson, put it.

Adrian, a journalist, wrote a beautifully written and amusing story of the "headache" that having a brain tumour may cause. His oligodendroglioma, a low-grade tumour that responds well to surgery, is not growing, which is a relief. He is currently working on a book that will describe his experience as a patient. Despite the constant uncertainty imposed by his tumour, he has discovered hitherto uncounted blessings. As he wrote in his published post, he was pleasantly grateful to have attained a level of knowledge that could have only come by confronting his own mortality. In this way, he claimed to have gained a "different perspective on life's values."

The ability to perceive the light and realise what is important can be a gift. Every day, my patients provide me with perspective on life's values.

I'll never forget stepping into an appointment room with heartbreaking news for my patient Sharon, a young mother in her early twenties who had flown to Baltimore from out of state with her husband, a soldier who had just returned from a tour of duty in Afghanistan. When the couple arrived at the clinic, we began by discussing their two children, a toddler and an infant, as well as the joys and challenges of parenting. When I recounted the operation and follow-up treatment for what I suspected was a high-grade, malignant tumour, Sharon was bright-eyed, attentive, and stoic. We were able to contact her primary care physician at home, put him on speaker phone, and determine a course of action for when she returned.

Technically, everything went down without a hitch in the OR. But, when I removed the tumour and sent it for an intraoperative test, it appeared to be just as deadly as I had suspected. A top pathologist arrived in the operating room to confirm that the initial flash-freeze report indicated a high-grade, malignant tumour. The last biopsy confirmed that it was one of the faster-growing, higher-grade GBM tumours.

During my post-op visit with Sharon and her husband, I first remarked on her bravery. "By the way, you look great today as you sit here." "What's your trick?"

"Brain surgery?" she asked, a hesitant smile on her face.

I next had to tell them that my darkest worries about the type of the tumour had been confirmed, as well as detail the best- and worst-case scenarios for life expectancy. Of course, we had therapy alternatives and would use them with caution. In such sessions with patients, I sometimes emphasise that numbers don't signify much and that putting a time restriction on how much time is left isn't useful. Sharon and her husband, on the other hand, insisted on understanding the basic expectations so that they could plan. I informed them that we would try to purchase more time and delay the inevitable; another year would be a blessing, but we would try for two more.

They recognized with sudden certainty that she was going to die at that time. Sharon then did something memorable for the rest of my life. She turned to face her husband, placed her hand on his knee, and while both of them sobbed, she gazed into his eyes and said softly but firmly, "I love you." She expressed everything with those three words: she knew he'd be left with two small children to raise without their mother, that he'd be alone for the rest of his life without his soul mate and companion. She was thinking of her loved ones at the time, not herself.

The pair returned six months later. Sharon was in a wheelchair, unable to walk due to the tumour's progression. We discussed practical issues, made the appropriate phone calls from the office to get her husband an extended leave from military duty, and called local agencies to arrange for home health care and child care.

As my two physician's assistants, Raven and Jill, and I said our goodbyes to Sharon and her husband, knowing that this was likely the final time we'd see her, we had to support each other.

"Whatever you need, call us," I reminded them. "You have my number, anytime."

What else could I possibly say? I didn't need to tell her to be strong because she was the one who taught her the lesson.

I was thinking about the recurring image in my life of the light beaming in the distance at the end of a dark tunnel, hallway, or a difficult climb as I saw Sharon's husband carry the weight of his approaching loss, nevertheless maintaining his military bearing as he pushed her wheelchair down the hall.

In the days and weeks that followed, I would think of Sharon, reminding myself of the privilege I have of witnessing patients' journeys, delving into their pasts, getting to know members of their families, imagining what it was like when their children were born and what it will be like when their loved one wakes in bed or stirs at their bedside and sees them take their last breath. This is the gift: to feel with them, even in their anguish, and to remember them forever.

10. Finding the Steel in Your Soul

As 2010 began, the week ending January 17 was brutal, demonstrating my long-held opinion that there are times when we just cannot resist nature and must accept our human limitations. However, the events of this week reminded me of the critical role that patients may play in their own healing, as well as the significant contribution they can make to the endeavour to understand brain cancer. To be fair, we were enjoying a respite from the huge blizzards that had descended on most of the country that January. But if any of us in the emergency services believed a few days of better weather would allow us to regain our breath, we were incorrect.

I had arranged for the evening off on Thursday afternoon, following two scheduled brain tumour procedures, so that Anna and I could drive to Washington, D.C., to attend a special ceremony honouring President Barack Obama. I had planned my day down to the minute, so that I could finish the most important task of the day and then, at the appointed time, change out of my scrubs, put on a tux, and rush out to the parking lot, where A-dressed in a gown for the occasion-would be waiting in the car. We'd make it to the capital in plenty of time if the weather held out.

The day had gone off without a hitch. My second patient, an elderly, knowledgeable gentleman with a tumour more dangerous than the one that killed Senator Edward Kennedy, cemented the day in my mind by saying something astonishing to me before surgery. Just before the anaesthesia kicked in, he called me over and said quietly, "I want to tell you something." "I want you to dig deep, and you will find the steel in your soul," he added, his voice mystical, his connection between the brain and the soul romantic. With every reason to be terrified, not knowing whether he would wake up, he had to place his confidence and his life in the hands of someone else. He asked me to explore myself, my brain, for the steel, to delve into the pieces that we all have, that make us what we are, who we are, and that allow us to overcome adversity. He didn't want me to make a mistake in this difficult instance. He was giving me some motivation!

His case was undoubtedly difficult, but as I frequently tell patients who ask me to describe my most difficult case, every case is the most difficult one I've ever handled at the time I'm in the OR. The old adage applies: it's not rocket science, but it is brain surgery. No matter how basic or straightforward the case, I am conscious that I am handling a human life and that the outcome is never definite.

Another patient had compared my profession as a brain surgeon to his career defusing improvised explosive devices and teaching Special Forces teams to identify homemade bombs, grenades, and land mines in seconds without losing their calm earlier in the week. When he awoke from surgery, he said, "You can do everything perfectly, perform in record time, make no errors, and still have it blow up in your face." "We have to be a little crazy to do it, you know?" he added. We must enjoy the thrill of adrenaline!"

While we brain surgeons have other motives for doing what we do (such as preventing loss of life and harm), perhaps we also get an adrenaline high from preventing another type of bomb from bursting in the OR.

On that Thursday, my first patient had taken longer to awaken than I was comfortable with, but had ultimately stirred and even cracked a joke, informing me after the removal of a massive 10-centimetre tumour, "I feel light-headed." But the person who had asked me to find the steel in my soul didn't seem to be awake. He finally opened his eyes. But before I could exhale a sigh of relief, we learned he had awoken unable to talk or move his right side, and we were in an emergency situation. With my heart racing, we discovered that he had suffered a severe seizure and that, according to a scan, a little blood clot in his brain was the likely cause. We were relieved when he woke up the second time and was able to speak and move his right side after rushing back to the OR to treat the clot. In fact, the next morning, he was back to walking and talking like he had before the procedure. But, in the interim, I was referred to an emergency case that needed to be treated that evening after we had just taken him out of the OR.

In the midst of this craziness, Anna called from the parking lot to check how much longer I'd be, and, of course, I wasn't ready. I felt terrible and apologised to her. When my second surgery of the day reached a crisis point, I had lost track of time and had forgotten to call her and tell her that our date night to the capital was not going to work out. She'd driven an hour in bad weather, and I was going to be late.

My devotion to my patients was wonderful for them, but no matter how philosophical Anna and I tried to be about the situation, it was not enjoyable for her. Too often, she bore the brunt of my surgical victories. I encouraged her to go to the dinner without me, knowing it would be an unforgettable experience, but Anna opted to save it for another time. So that was the end of our excitement about having a date on a weeknight.

Working till the early morning hours, I thought that we had paid our dues with the day's earlier difficult instances and that the next case would be easier. Not so. Our next patient was a young family man, a top-level executive at a large software firm, who had been unexpectedly struck by a big tumour that had a mind of its own when we went into surgery. The tumour refused to come out, causing blood to gush and pour all over the operating table while my senior resident, Dr. Shaan Raza, and I bobbed and weaved to avoid the strikes that kept coming. When my patient's condition stabilised, he performed admirably both postoperatively and subsequently on. Given the dangers he had faced, this was nothing short of a miracle.

The next morning, a Saturday, I was getting ready to leave after doing rounds a little early, having set aside time that afternoon to work on a review of Schmidek and Sweet's Operative Neurosurgical Techniques, when I was alerted that a helicopter was on its way carrying a patient in critical condition due to a massive haemorrhage in the brain.

In seconds, one of my fourth-year residents and I were flying down the hallway of the Johns Hopkins Bayview Medical Center, followed closely by two other members of the Q Team. Paramedics stormed out the hospital's exit doors into the chilly January morning to meet the arriving helicopter and transfer my patient to a gurney.

Waiting just inside, I analysed the CT scan results on my laptop computer, mentally planning out a surgical strategy for the patient, a fifty-two-year-old developmentally handicapped man with a moderate head injury. The enormous blood clot that had formed was forcing his brain to inflate like a balloon and threatened to push out his brain stem, killing him instantly.

As the paramedics transported the unconscious, already-intubated patient inside the hospital, we met the gurney. My team and I seized command, rushing down the corridor and into the OR, with medical personnel stationed to direct all other traffic. Once the patient was ready for surgery, we needed to move quickly—first to remove a large bone flap, then to suction the blood clot, evacuate fluids, weld shut the no-longer-clotted vessel, and secure other vessels in the area, all while ensuring that the rest of his body's functions continued to function normally. Finishing just in time, I heard an almost audible exhale from everyone in the OR as we realised we were in the clear. My patient quickly awoke, eyes wide open!

I have to agree with my bomb-disposal patient that sometimes you need to be a little crazy to work in our fields. However, there is a method to the chaos. In fact, in order to avoid going insane, I had lately devised some novel techniques to employ comedy and competition to lift people's spirits on difficult days. One of my faves was an ongoing arm-wrestling match among the ranks of the Q Team, in which contender after contender tried to beat me.

The championship struggle began one day when one of the very fit young residents claimed that I was past my prime.

"Are you sure you want a piece of me?" As I prepared for the match, I cautioned him. "I may be forty-two years old, but under these scrubs, I'm rippling with muscles of steel!"

My doctor suggested that what I had under my scrubs could be "not fully mature stem cells—waiting to be developed." But I had a few Kaliman gimmicks up my sleeve. I knew the trick was to lean your body into the job. Bingo! To everyone's surprise, including mine, I won.

A series of challenges by some of the buff young bucks on staff ensued, with the events attracting big crowds of surgical staff, students, lab technicians, and nurses. I soon had to resort to mental gymnastics to avoid being crushed as I faced increasingly muscle-bound challengers—and after Anna pointedly inquired what would happen if I shattered my arm or hand.

During a bout in the cafeteria lobby with an extremely muscular medical student, I was able to use one of my more effective techniques. "Let me win!" I said quietly to myself just before we started, acting absolutely assured. Fortunately, he agreed. But I wasn't convinced that future opponents would be as gracious, so I resorted to stalling, telling anyone who challenged me, "You aren't in good enough shape yet," and then adding, "Let me know when you're ready."

Nothing makes me feel more compelled to improve our research than witnessing young patients, who should have their entire life ahead of them, have their time cut short. Aaron Watson was one of these patients.

Aaron and his sister, Ava, were raised by their father, Paul Watson, and all three became close family members of mine. Aaron was the prototypical golden kid, a young African-American Adonis and music prodigy whose trumpet playing had caught Wynton Marsalis' notice at the age of twelve. Aaron's prowess on the football field had earned him a statewide Unsung Hero award for his achievements with his team during his first year of college. Above all, he was a cheerful, optimistic human being with a bright future ahead of him.

Then, when Aaron was eighteen, he had a relapse of health problems that appeared to be tied to football injuries. Aaron saw a paediatric surgeon in July 2005, the month I arrived at Hopkins, for bilateral shoulder instability and underwent surgery on the right side. Everything returned to normal, but he began experiencing headaches and double vision in early November. No one was concerned because he had a history of migraines dating back to the age of twelve or so. However, a few months later, he began to have discomfort in his left shoulder that radiated through his left side, as well as severe, persistent migraines that kept him up at night. By the next summer, the headaches no longer felt like migraines, and he was not just losing weight but also vomiting. He was discovered to have lost thirty pounds in five months in November 2006, and his double vision had returned. A facial X-ray at another hospital's emergency room came out normal, and he was given pain medicine. When the medication didn't help his double vision, he went to a paediatrician, despite the fact that he was only nineteen years old, who began to connect the dots when he evaluated Aaron's symptoms.

An MRI on November 15, 2006, revealed a big tumour behind his eye. We finally met two days later, when I concluded Aaron's brain was in risk of herniating and rushed him to the OR. Despite my unwillingness to speculate on what I saw in the movies, I informed him, his father, and sister that the surgery would be dangerous and complicated due to the tumour's location. Aaron arrived prepared to fight. Though the tumour was firmly infiltrated in his brain, we attempted to remove as much of it as possible without leaving him with deficiencies; on that score, I was certain that he would feel significantly better when he awoke.

Sure enough, Aaron emerged from the operating room and awoke like a champion, his headaches gone. But when I looked at the tumour tissue under the microscope and discovered it was a GBM, I realised this was only the first round of surgery.

Aaron, his sister, and his father all had varied emotions to learn about the sort of tumour and the accompanying fight strategy, which included chemo and radiation. "But I feel so much better," Aaron said, mostly in denial. Why?" Ava had reared her young brother virtually as a surrogate mother, and she was saddened, undoubtedly aware of the difficult road ahead. And Paul was stoic, implying that even though he knew what was coming, he needed to keep his emotions in check and conserve his energy.

If we were lucky, Aaron would have six months of good health.

Instead, we received three months of him feeling somewhat better, followed by the finding that not only was the tumour still growing, but a cyst had formed in his brain. During this time, Paul and Ava were concerned about the drastic changes in Aaron's personality brought on by the pressure in his frontal brain. Aaron's sweet, sunny, calm personality vanished, and he became belligerent, defiant, and aloof, frequently failing to show up for or care about follow-up visits and partying excessively, either to avoid pain or due to lowered inhibitions. In October 2007, I returned Aaron to the OR to treat the cyst and determine what the tumour was doing inside his brain.

Paul's eyes were filled with pain as he brought his son into the operating room for the second time, as if he didn't want to let go. But, once again, Aaron's life force was so strong that he awoke feeling like his old self, at least for the next month or two. Then, gradually, the slide toward the end began.

Throughout this time, Paul had been on his own roller coaster. After achieving success as a financial investment analyst, he decided to devote all of his energies to caring for Aaron, exactly when he was at the top of his game and his children had grown up and gone out of the house. Paul re-housed his son and stayed by his side until his final gloomy days, spending his savings in the process. In March 2008, Paul was basically homeless after burying his kid.

"I don't really know where to begin, so I'll just start," Paul wrote after Aaron died. As you might guess, this has been one of the most difficult periods of my life. I truly miss my son. I would lie next to him and converse during his final week on this earth with us. Sometimes I don't know what to say except "I love you" and "I'll see you again." Being his father was an honour and a gift from God."

I was outraged while Paul and Ava were grieving. We weren't doing enough in our field to respond quickly enough to save lives. The first thing I said to Paul after he booked an appointment to see me that summer was, "Your son didn't have to die."

Paul, an African-American guy who appeared to be younger than his middle age and was insightful, deeply intellectual, and tastefully dressed, was deep into his own effort to make sense of a world flipped upside down. He had, however, promised Aaron that his death would not be in vain. "In Aaron's last days with us, I would say that I didn't understand why this was happening to him," Paul explained. The only reason I could think of was that his death would allow others to survive."

Paul Watson returned to visit me a short time later to outline his plan to keep his promise to his son. He and Ava had drafted the documents to establish the Brain Cancer Research for a Cure Foundation. He informed me that as soon as word got out about the plan, his phone started ringing with offers of assistance. He was also back at work and doing much better financially. "I feel Aaron looking over this effort and blessing it in surprising ways every day."

He and Ava had put at the top of the flyer for the foundation's dedication ceremony, "Remembering a life taken by brain cancer by creating hope for those living with it." The Watsons expressed their hope in the foundation's mission statement to "create a better quality of life for brain cancer patients by increasing public awareness and making quantum leaps in scientific research" and "to one day be able to give a brain cancer patient the news that they have a condition that will not control them but can be controlled." I was inspired by their commitment to use Aaron's death for good, as did the rest of my team when Paul and Ava came to the Friday night meeting to share their tale and describe their intentions.

Every patient's narrative, tragic or triumphant, is unique. But, as we learn more, we realise that brain tumours, whether benign or malignant, low or high grade, are equal-opportunity offenders with no borders, attacking victims of all ages, ethnic and socioeconomic backgrounds, and nations. The more patients and their families that participate in our work at the lab, whether by attending our Friday meetings, speaking in public forums, or giving tissue and brain fluid samples, the more empowered we all are.

Don Rottman, a patient and good friend of mine, exemplifies the significance of patient involvement in the fight against brain cancer. Don has also stated that, despite the devastation of his diagnosis, he would not trade away the lessons he has learned about himself, love, and life as a result of his experience. Throughout our four years of getting to know one another, I've often thought about how similar our temperaments and energy levels are. Don and I are both in our early forties, both driven—albeit in separate fields—outdoorsmen, fishermen, and students of literature and philosophy. Don was born and raised in Baltimore and comes from a blue-collar family. He planned to go to college, but due to financial constraints, he ended up in the military. He advanced through the ranks of the army while also part-time studying and worked his way through various libraries. When he left the military, which had led him to places such as Panama and Costa Rica, he spoke great Spanish and proceeded to work for an international organisation that trained teams in developing and sometimes war-torn countries.

Don was divorced, the father of a fourteen-year-old daughter, and a self-avowed workaholic when I first met him in June 2007. Don, a wealthy businessman, had his first feeling that something wasn't right when he was out of town making a presentation at a conference. He explained, "I kept hitching my words."

"Hitching?"

"I'd open my mouth and nothing would come out. I wondered if there was something odd, but hoped no one else would notice. I believed I was doing a good job of concealing it." However, he was unable to talk again when he went out to supper with friends. He could hear the words in his head and taste them in his mouth again, but nothing came out. While his companions respectfully disregarded his dilemma, he recovered and went on. "When I got my faculties back," Don went on to say, "I said that I was going to go to the gym to work out." When a couple of his coworkers went to meet him at the gym and he didn't show up, one of the women in the group became concerned, saying, "Don Rottman is never late." Meanwhile, neighbours in Don's hotel room heard weird noises and alerted hotel security when he didn't answer their knock on the door. Don was discovered in his workout clothes, convulsing on the floor, in full seizure, of which he later recalled nothing.

After five seizures, Don awoke a day and a half later in a nearby tiny regional hospital. Although the emergency room doctors were not specialists, they were able to tell from his MRI that he had a tumour and encouraged him to see a neurosurgeon as soon as possible.

When Don's usual doctor returned to Baltimore a few days later and saw the MRI, he got quite worried and recommended him to Dr. Cliff Solomon in Annapolis, a highly respected, prominent surgeon and a good friend of mine. Dr. Solomon told Don after viewing the films, "There are few people in the world who could even touch you... You're extremely fortunate because one of the few brain surgeons capable of doing this works right here at Hopkins."

And this is when Don's and my paths crossed. He was motivated to overcome the difficulties and wanted to be a part of the larger struggle from the start. At first, I believed that the tumour would turn out to be harmless. But, before we could do the necessary operation, we needed many MRIs over a few months to map out where his speech and movement functions were located in his brain. I asked Don for a favour after the operation was planned, with Dr. Solomon attending.

The makers of PBS's NOVA series were interested in filming a story about my work as a surgeon/scientist, and they specifically requested footage of an awake craniotomy, which is what I would be performing on Don. When I asked if he would consider having his surgery filmed, he might have easily denied or taken a few days to think about it, considering the level of terror that any patient experiences before surgery, let alone how he could feel about having his brain shown to the world. Instead, Don replied, "Absolutely, I'm in." From the start, he realised that his decision to accept his trip was not only for himself, but also for others, many of whom are as clueless as he was about what goes on within their thoughts. Don proved to be the show's star. We activated his brain in the operating room by using a map that showed us the areas that controlled his lip movement, hand movement, and speech capabilities. We could determine where he created words and where he observed visuals while he was awake and able to speak, as well as where areas of his brain were triggered by specific inquiries. I was certain that with Don as our navigator, we could complete this challenging surgery and bring him out without any complications.

I thanked Don again throughout the procedure for consenting to donate some of his tissue and brain fluids to our lab for research.

Don responded without skipping a beat, "Take as much as you need," causing the entire film team to laugh.

Don's only gripes were the inconvenience of being chained to the table for so long and the inability to drink coffee. We finally finished, but as he began drumming his fingers in anticipation of being unbolted, he discovered that he couldn't move them anymore, and soon after, he couldn't move his arm—all of this happening in front of our eyes so swiftly that we couldn't stop the setback. We transported him to the neurosurgery intensive care unit so that a neurology team could examine him. The conclusion was that his arm's damage was likely transient and that he would regain much of its function once his brain adjusted and rewired itself.

I stopped up with him later, during a coffee break, to see how he was doing.

"Fine," Don said emphatically. "But I really need some coffee!"

"Here," I said, "have yours." It's the very least I can do for you."

The biopsy, which should have taken no more than five days, took the pathology lab three weeks. When I finally got the findings, I was disappointed to see that we were dealing with an anaplastic astrocytoma-a malignancy grade lower than glioblastoma and not the news Don or I wanted to hear. The tumour was star-shaped, with tentacles that connected different sections of the brain, and it was made up of many different types of cells, which explained why it had been so difficult to study. Don was Muhammad Ali to my Dr. Ferdie Pacheco, and we went after it hard. Don never missed a day of work during his combination radiation and chemotherapy treatments. The most difficult conversation we had was when we met in my office with his sister, Amy, to assess his condition after six months of treatment-almost a year after discovering the tumour. We were still dealing with the unknown, but his tumour had not grown back. Don was curious about his life expectancy.

"You know, numbers don't tell us everything," that's what I said. "Everybody is different, and we have no idea how you'll fare in the big picture." When Don and Amy said they still wanted to know the odds, I told them that 50% of patients survive between two and five years, but I quickly added, "The reality is that you are not a number." "You are a person."

Amy burst into tears. Don was emotional as well, although it appeared that he was more shocked than anything else. I proposed that we concentrate on that as long as he was healthy and things were looking up. I reminded Don of what he and other patients had taught me-to approach life not by preparing to die but by deciding how to live the rest of your life. Don Rottman swiftly set down a course to represent such a mentality.

Before long, he became an impassioned, tireless spokesperson for the work of the lab, deploying his considerable writing and speaking skills to tell people what he had learned when his disease forced him to be vulnerable-not his strong suit before being T-boned by brain cancer, a metaphor that I have used often since he introduced it. He also wrote eloquently on the impact of his diagnosis on his relationship with his teenage daughter, the light of his life: "Tori's first question to me after I discussed my disease with her was, 'How long did they tell you that you had to live, Dad?' And my response was perhaps the most improper and the most stupid answer that I could have given her; I simply fell into tears, not because of my anxiety or my personal anguish for myself but what I felt I was doing to her. She accepted my response better than any adult could have. She walked over to me and hugged me and promised me she will be alright."

Anna and I have never tried to separate our social networks from our extended Hopkins family, and she has become as fond of Don as I am. He would have become a buddy regardless of how I met him because he was a kindred spirit who would not back down from a challenge. Don Rottman has not given up the fight three years after being diagnosed. With all of his trench labour, he could definitely get a medical degree. He has also been an invaluable resource for newly diagnosed patients, inspiring many of them to become engaged with the lab, whether through fund-raising or raising public awareness of brain tumours.

Don, Paul Watson, and his daughter, Ava, as well as many of my patients and their loved ones who contribute to our lab and its work, make me feel as though I'm not doing enough. When I see how far the lab has come in such a short period of time, it proves that we can achieve so much more if we set our eyes higher and find the steel in our souls to pursue them. One of my favourite "spare-time" tasks is to analyse morbidity rates in different populations using the great National Institutes of Health databases, which are free to download but receive little use. We need to start investigating families where cancer runs in families and look for probable genetic or environmental reasons. What enables one patient to defy the odds while leaving another without the resources to avoid or overcome a disease?

Though we have yet to verify this scientifically, patients who actively participate in the search for a cure for brain cancer appear to be more hopeful and to have better overall health. Similarly, hopeful scientists and medics are compelled to go the extra mile in their pursuit for answers.

At this point, I have wonderful news to share about the character of the current and future generations of students that I teach—whether in the lecture hall, during clinic hours, in the OR, in the laboratory, or in any of the numerous venues that I've had the pleasure of seeing as a professor. For me, teaching has come full circle. For one thing, my focus during my studies in Mexico was on becoming a teacher, a desire that I was unable to realise. For another, teaching allows me to advocate the next generation of physicians and scientists in the same vein as the many mentors who aided my development—some of whom I scarcely knew but who opened doors for me that would not have opened otherwise.

Dr. Joe L. Martinez, the director of the Marine Biological Laboratory in Woods Hole, Massachusetts, invited me to teach a weeklong course in human brain anatomy at the Summer Program in Neuroscience, Ethics, and Survival (SPINES).

What do you say when your mentor, one of the brightest brains in the field of neuroscience of learning and memory, bestows such an award on you? If you're like me, your question is, "When do I begin?" "Let's go rock 'n' roll!"

Aside from wanting to work with Joe, I couldn't pass up the opportunity to include a fantastic family vacation in Woods Hole, right on the ocean, across from Nantucket and Martha's Vineyard—a place that would become a home away from home for one week every summer at the historic Marine Biological Lab, built in the 1800s.

When discussing the course curriculum with Professor Martinez, I expressed my desire to take an alternative approach and make the week memorable for the many scientific undergraduates that attended the program. Joe listened to my idea without reacting in his customary brusque manner until I explained, in brief, that I wanted to go the extra mile to bring in cadavers and human brains.

Joe burst out laughing. "You've come a long way!" he exclaimed, before recalling how terrified I had been the first time I dissected a body during Stanford's Dia de los Muertos. Well, I was living proof of education's power.

My students at Woods Hole were captivated by our use of cadavers and the experience of holding brains, dissecting them, and inspecting tissue under the microscope, just as I had imagined. For those who were concerned, I hired a very helpful chief lab assistant in 2009 who assured them that if she could overcome her fear of this task, anyone could. Who was this convincing assistant? Gabriella Quinones, ten, who, I might say, stole the show.

The week in Woods Hole is also as close to a honeymoon as Anna and I will have for a while, even with our kids and the company of the SPINES students and teachers. Time slows down, and for the first time in a long time, I am not in a rush. Anna and I manage to fit in some romantic walks by the ocean as well as dinner and a glass of wine with the help of skilled babysitters. Perhaps it's the wine and the food, but Anna always appears to suggest I'm onto something when I look into her green eyes and tell her about my latest idea!

Of course, I have my down days when I can't seem to find the steel in my spirit. But I always return to the reality that I have survived a few close calls and am still alive to tell the tale and do my work, and this thinking motivates me to continue on my road.

In recent years, I've realised that, aside from a desire to find a cure for brain cancer, there's something else that drives me-something bigger: the quest to understand, through this work, how we can use our abilities to do a better job of being good to each other, as my father admonished me years ago. Perhaps the actions we must take to improve the world for humanity and learn to treat one another with more care are not that dissimilar to those required to stop brain cancer. Certainly, we must increase awareness about the societal diseases that divide and separate us, feed hatred, and stigmatise people who are different and underrepresented. Certainly, equitable access to quality care is a value on which we can all agree, even if we disagree on how to achieve it. We all benefit when we don't limit chances for everyone who wants to pursue his or her aspirations.

In spiritual terms, these thoughts make me question how our understanding of the brain can help us better understand the grand order of the universe-and the moral lessons that God may be attempting to teach us. After studying the miracle that is the brain, it's impossible for me not to believe in God-or whatever name one chooses. Every day, it's impossible not to feel as if a higher force is guiding me, keeping me modest and grounded in the conviction that what we do here on Earth has meaning. My faith also serves as a reminder that there are aspects of life and death over which I have no control, as well as a means of accepting that the terra firma I have sought my entire life is not a real place at all.

To be sure, if we stopped crossing borders and jumping barriers in our quest for more stable ground-personally, scientifically, and spiritually-the human race would cease to exist. But, in order to unravel the mysteries of the voyage, we must continue on our journey through life, seeking the light of answers that may sometimes be out of grasp.

One enigma I may never solve is how we keep going when everything appears to be going wrong. What ignited the fighter within me during those moments when death was closing in? And what enables my patients to progress and find joy despite the most bleak prognosis? I return to Ken Zabel's unwavering belief that we are all part of a larger purpose.

Following Zabels' first appearance at our lab meeting, I saw Ken for a third and final surgery-"our last round," as he called it. Ken was unconcerned. "God has a plan," he went on to say.

Raven Morris went to meet Ken and Betty in pre-op on the morning of his third surgery to examine Ken's recognition of the same selection of words and images that he had used before his first procedure almost a year previously. Raven realized around halfway through the test that Ken couldn't identify common images and was having difficulty reading some of the easy words. She strolled into the hall and beckoned me, saying, "He missed eighty-five percent of the time." "What do you intend to do?"

I conducted a preliminary review. Ken's lecture was moving quickly. He was having difficulty identifying a "owl," mistaking it for a "bird." "Oh, I know, it's a..." he'd say, only to be puzzled by an image of an umbrella or a table.

"Ken," I explained. "If you don't mind, we'll put you to sleep for this surgery." I wouldn't be doing you justice if I asked you to stay awake." He agreed and performed admirably. We were able to relieve a lot of pressure on his brain, and his speech was improving days later.

He returned to work for a month after surgery and provided himself speech treatment on the job, using a blackboard and homemade flash cards. But his language and coordination began to deteriorate almost immediately. Betty informed him that she would be in charge of the office and that he needed to rest. When she contacted me to inform me of the change, I decided to try to arrange a meeting with him before too much time elapsed. I don't make many house calls, but with Ken no longer able to fly from Florida to Baltimore, I felt compelled to pay him a visit. Part of my decision to go stemmed from our special bond and everything I had drawn from his positive attitude-his proud, courageous focus on battling the dragon; the sight of him brokering deals on his laptop in the ICU six hours after surgery; and the audacious way he had become my patient in the first place. Another reason I wanted to see Ken was to reconnect with my early motivation to become a doctor, which had been passed down via my family. After all, this was what my Nana Maria used to do when she made house calls. Something told me to go-another rite of passage was approaching.

The fact was that when Betty contacted me about Ken's decline, I was at a crossroads in my life and work. I could feel my spirits sagging as the underdog, a part I purposely play so that I may remain humble and work harder every day, after a string of patients died from brain cancer. Though self-doubt is a frequent force in pushing myself up to increase the fight, I was so low at the time that I questioned if I should continue. Perhaps seeing my hero Ken Zabel would provide me with a much-needed boost of energy-the motivation to keep going.

I flew down to Florida and spent the day with the Zabels after clearing my schedule. Despite my heartbreak at the potential of losing this magnificent, noble patient and the sadness and loss his wife and children would experience, the day turned out to be a beautiful one in many respects, and I was once again impressed by Ken's spiritual presence.

He was still the big muscular person he had been before his sickness, and the cancer had not taken away his contagious smile and easy going demeanour. He was ashamed to admit that he needed to go to the bathroom but didn't want to use the bedpan.

"Well, then, let's go pee," I proposed. "You are not required to be modest. I've seen your brain a couple times nude."

He let me carry him to the bathroom while laughing, and as he stood there stark naked, with me trying to hold up all two hundred pounds of him, he couldn't urinate.

"Why don't we just turn on the water?" I proposed. But all this did was make me feel compelled to go! "Ken, you'd better go, because if you don't, I'm going to wet my pants!"

We were soon all laughing and having a good time. Ken was in such good spirits that he wanted to spend some time in the living room. Instead of dressing, he put a sheet over himself like a Roman toga. Sitting there while we talked, with me carrying most of the discussion and him occasionally chipping in with amusing comments, he reminded me of a noble Roman warrior, like Caesar nearing the end of his reign, vulnerable and withering. Ken hugged me several times before I had to go. Even though I was the one leaving his house, I had the impression that he was already departing this world, travelling down a tunnel and glancing back over his shoulder, as if he had anything else to say. He motioned for me to approach him. He said I was his idol, but I had to disagree and tell him, "You're my hero."

With nothing else to say, I resumed my walk, and he drew me closer to him to say something I wasn't sure I got at first.

"You are so rich."

The sky was pitch black and starless when I returned to Baltimore late at night and drove from the airport to our neighbourhood, out near a remote portion of the suburbs with few streetlamps. Nonetheless, I imagined myself on the roof of Palaco, feeling as if the entire starry sky was mine. Yes, I was wealthy!

The silence of the world comforted me as I considered the loneliness of the journey from life over the border to the next area where we can only walk on our own.

The stillness of the night gave me time to reflect on the action-packed day that lied ahead as I drove on. During clinic hours, who would I meet new patients with intriguing and inspiring journeys? What discoveries are my students and residents likely to share with me? What might happen in the lab and in the operating room tomorrow to help us defeat the beast of brain cancer? Even getting the chance to ask the questions made me feel like the happiest man on the planet.

Then I remembered what Santiago Ramón y Cajal said about luck. Borrowing from a Spanish proverb, he stated that luck in scientific inquiry, like in life, comes to those who look for it rather than those who seek it. Thomas Jefferson, the founding father of my adopted country, may have said it even better: "I'm a great believer in luck, and I find that the harder I work, the more I have of it."

Printed in Dunstable, United Kingdom

66216554R00097